THE MAJOR ISSUES LECTURE SERIES
is made possible through a grant from
International Telephone and Telegraph Corporation

This series of lectures was held at
the Graduate School of Management of the University of California,
Los Angeles.

LARGE CORPORATIONS IN A CHANGING SOCIETY

J. Fred Weston, *Editor*
Graduate School of Management, UCLA

With a Foreword by
Harold S. Geneen

New York: New York University Press   1974

Preface

Dean Harold M. Williams

This volume is part of a broader Research Program in Business and Society of the Graduate School of Management, UCLA. It specifically reflects the research developed over a period of years in the Research Program in Competition and Business Policy under the direction of Professor J. Fred Weston and communicates some of the findings of its continued research efforts to a more general audience.

We are far from having the answers to many of the fundamental questions raised. We have not yet developed a full understanding or delineation of the proper role of the large firm as an important corporate citizen in our society. We do recognize that decisions in large corporate organizations must be made with reference to a number of different interests in society and by more ambiguous criteria than have been employed in the past. Self-interest can no longer be the sole or primary guiding principle for corporate decision-making. But then, what principles are to be used as guides?

These principles will not be readily or easily developed. Development calls for a deeper appreciation of the needs and contributions of each of the interests in our society and their relationships to each other. Above all, it calls for greater reasoning and less emoting, more comprehension and less reaction on the part of all interests.

Hopefully, the essays in this volume will contribute to progress in developing an increased understanding of the role of the large corporate enterprise in society. We express our appreciation to the International Telephone and Telegraph Corporation for financial support of the lecture series which has made this volume possible. Marion Klein assisted in the organization of the lecture series and in the editing of this volume.

Foreword

Harold S. Geneen

Chairman and Chief Executive Officer
International Telephone and Telegraph Corporation

The subject matter—"Large Corporations in a Changing Society"
—is, in itself, a rather large-scale undertaking—a topic that reaches
out to every corner of the globe and contains information of concern to
just about everyone. This book will hopefully provide broader expo-
sure for facts as opposed to rhetoric and, thus, counteract the growing
tendency of many Americans to sit back and allow the "headlines" to
rule their thought processes. By this I mean, relying on capsule de-
scription for detailed coverage of the day's news events, or limiting
reading selections to the best-seller lists ... or, allowing the
well-entrenched economic theories of the past to stand without peri-
odic critical reexamination in light of newly developed technology or
rapidly changing societal and economic facts of life.

Unfortunately, too many of us seem to be joining a sort of superficial society that casually tosses aside the finely-honed tools of higher education and the freedom to challenge and to offer constructive criticism, and to make efforts to significantly improve the quality of life. We need to counteract the growing tendency of many Americans to sit back and allow the spokesmen for various causes to do their thinking for them.

But we should not accept traditional standards or theories at face value. We must reexamine and retest to find out whether traditional approaches to a problem are still valid. If so, fine. If not, we have to broaden the traditional approach to industrial economics and reevaluate the role of large-scale enterprise.

Participation in programs such as this one is indicative of ITT's tremendous concern for stimulating greater communication and cooperation among economic thinkers and the people who set economic policy. Cynics will point to our "vested interest." But each and every one of us has a similar vested interest in our mutual ultimate goal of insuring efficient allocation of earth's limited resources to provide the greatest possible benefit to humanity.

Contents

PART III: THE CORPORATE ECONOMY AND PUBLIC POLICY

The Major Issues Lecture Series held at the University of California, Los Angeles, was an eight part analysis of current and emerging issues on the role of "Large Corporations in a Changing Society."
The following nationally known authorities participated in this topical series:

Oscar Grusky, *Professor*
Department of Sociology, UCLA
"Evaluating Organizations"
Symbols versus reality in measuring effectiveness

Marc L. Nerlove, *Professor*
Department of Economics, of Chicago University
"Household and Economy: *Toward a New Theory of Population and Economic Growth"*
Implications of long-run economic trends for space-ship earth

Oliver E. Williamson, *Professor*
Department of Economics, University of Pennsylvania
"Assessing the Modern Corporation: Transaction Cost Considerations"
Efficiency of the firm and the market system

Richard A. Posner, *Professor*
School of Law, University of Chicago
"Power in America: The Role of the Large Corporation"
The diversity of influences in a pluralistic society

Sidney M. Robbins, *Professor*
Graduate School of Business, Columbia University
and
Robert B. Stobaugh, *Professor*
Graduate School of Business Administration, Harvard University
"Some Financial Dilemmas of the Multinational Enterprise"
Thriving or surviving in the turbulent international financial environment

Neil H. Jacoby, *Professor*
Graduate School of Management, UCLA
"Myths of the Corporate Economy"
The distribution of power in a pluralistic society

Michael Granfield, Professor
Graduate School of Management, UCLA
"Concentrated Industries and Economic Performance"
Analysis of profitability patterns among the largest corporations

Ronald H. Coase, Editor
Journal of Law & Economics
Professor, University of Chicago
"Economists and Public Policy"
Social costs and social benefits

PART I

Organizations
in Society

Large scale organizations are characteristic of modern urban indus-trial society. We experience large scale organizations in business, gov-ernment, religion, medical care, correctional institutions, and so forth. Large-scale organizations of all kinds have an increasingly great im-pact on our lives, whether good or bad. In part, large-scale organiza-tions result from their greater efficiency. But some people are con-cerned that large scale organizations may also result from the exercise of power by large organizations seeking to become larger. A lost sense of participation and identity has resulted from the increasing impact of large organizations.

Concerns about the large and increasing size of business organiza-tions have been especially great. Issues have been raised with regard to the share of the economy represented by the largest 100 or 200 firms and of the share of the top 4 or 8 firms in individual markets. Also the number of billion-dollar corporations has been rising.

Concomittantly, other effects of urban industrial society have been increasingly felt. The air is less pure. The transportation arteries are more crowded. For some, work is less satisfying and the work ethic less compelling. To what extent is the large corporation the cause of the deterioration of the environment and of the "quality of social life"?

The issues posed are complex and are not easily answered with solid evidence or analysis. Simplistic answers that large corporations are either an unmitigated evil or the pristine product of the operation of an invisible hand and immutable economic laws are doubtless invalid. Doctrinaire criticisms or doctrinaire defenses are not helpful.

Our goal is to understand better the role of large business organizations. Where their scope can be reduced or limited without economic or social costs, it should be. Where limits on large firms would involve economic and social losses, we should know the tradeoffs—what do we gain and what do we lose. Informed public opinion and rational public policy can be formulated soundly only on the basis of such knowledge.

This volume attempts to make a contribution to an increased understanding of the modern corporation in American society. Our inquiry is divided into three parts:

I. Organizations in Society
II. Corporate Power and Control
III. The Corporate Economy and Public Policy

Part I seeks to provide a broad framework and perspective for viewing the large corporation. Part II analyzes the nature of the internal governance of corporations and their external powers in both the domestic and international environments. Part III presents factual evidence on corporate activities and discusses their implications for public policy in the economic sphere.

In the first part of the book two papers are included. The first paper, by Professor Grusky, presents a broad framework for evaluating organizations in a broad sociological context. The paper by Professor Nerlove reexamines the nature of the household and its future to determine whether there are likely to be any impacts from this direction on the size, nature, and functioning of the firm. The contents of each of these papers are discussed briefly in order to orient their materials to the particular issues that are the focus of this book.

Professor Grusky observes that evaluation of corporate and other organizations is a central process in our society. This suggests that the large corporate organizations cannot assume that their existence is their own self-justification. Furthermore, organizations exist in an environment of other organizations, and there is a broad competitive framework that transcends economic organizations in which all parts of society interact.

An organization may be said to be effective if it obtains resources for functioning well, but is also conserving resources or has flexibility for obtaining additional resources so that it can adapt to new circumstances in the future. But the effectiveness of an organization in a larger sense depends on the criteria applied, and this, in turn, will depend at least in part on the group affiliations and ideology of the evaluator. The implication of this for business firms is that the criteria it may apply for measuring effectiveness will not necessarily be the same criteria that society applies.

Professor Grusky sets forth five criteria applicable to all kinds of organizations: (1) Output Indicators, (2) Satisfaction Indicators, (3) Throughput Indicators, (4) Adaptation Indicators, and (5) Leadership Indicators. In the application of these criteria Professor Grusky observes that three assumptions often made are invalid. The first assumption is that organizations have a single objective and that the evaluation of performance can be made with regard to that one reference point. The second assumption is that the requirements of effective organization are so unambiguous as to easily obtain a consensus or general agreement as to what defines an effective organization. A third assumption is that an organization itself can fully determine its level of effectiveness. Professor Grusky emphasizes that an organization's effectiveness is to a considerable extent determined by society's criteria, not by the criteria of the individual organization.

These observations are particularly relevant for business organizations. Of the five criteria set forth by Professor Grusky, business firms have typically placed almost exclusive emphasis on the first—output indicators. This has been expressed as "getting results." In general, corporations have emphasized output, throughput, and adaptation measures. Satisfaction indicators both from the standpoint of individuals involved in the organization and from the standpoint of social criteria have only recently begun to engage the attention of corporate enterprise. Leadership indicators, Professor Grusky observes, when considered, have tended to be subjectively and unsystematically examined.

Thus, Professor Grusky provides a necessary broad framework for evaluating organizations, including the corporate enterprise on which this volume focuses. Therefore, when in subsequent papers and in other discussions of the corporation, economic criteria alone are emphasized, we must acknowledge that a complete evaluation has not been made. This broad framework is therefore useful in providing additional criteria and indicating additional directions in which evidence must be gathered for a complete evaluation of tradeoffs in connection with formulating public policy toward corporate enterprise.

In the second paper, Professor Nerlove develops a theory of economic growth through an understanding of the way investment in human capital increases the value of human time. This in turn effects the relative costs and prices confronting U.S. households in their decisions on the number and quality of children they produce. He defines the four basic elements of the "New Home Economics," as follows: (1) a utility function with arguments which are not physical commodities, but home-produced bundles of attributes; (2) a household production function technology; (3) an external labor market environment providing the means for transforming household resources into market commodities; and (4) a set of household resource constraints.

The utility function is defined from the standpoint of a single decision maker whose decisions govern all members of the family. The production function involves inputs of time and market-purchasable commodities. These inputs are used to produce within the household the goods and services that in turn lead to satisfaction. The external labor market environment involves the terms upon which household members can enter the labor market, the wages they can earn, and the prices at which market commodities can be purchased. The fourth element, the resources used in the household, include time and other nonwage income. But in addition, Professor Nerlove emphasizes the quality of time resources and the quality of other family resources—both genetic and material—passed from one generation to the next. In its simplest form the theory holds that two time inputs (husband's and wife's) and one general market-purchasable commodity are assumed to produce three household goods: namely, child number, child quality, and a general commodity called "other satisfactions."

The timing and spacing of children, the opportunities for part-time work, accumulations of lifetime labor market experience, and choices as to the amount of education to be invested in all revolve heavily on the terms under which women can participate in the labor market and thus share in the transformation of the household's time resources into market commodities. A rise in the cost of a mother's time for the family will cause substitution away from time-intensive goods such as children, and toward those activities in the household requiring more inputs of market-purchasable commodities.

The composition of a family is strongly associated with the female labor force participation. Professor Nerlove observes that children, especially younger children, are time intensive as compared with other goods produced in the home. Unless the increasing investment of human capital increases the marginal productivity of a unit of time in the care and rearing of children in an offsetting fashion, increases in the value of time will lead to a shift away from children to less time-intensive activities.

Thus the income effect of the increase in value of human time should lead to a substitution of quality (that is, more spent on education of children) for quantity of children, as well as leading to a substitution away from children altogether to less time-intensive goods. Investments in child quality may take two major forms: (1) sound nutrition and health care; and (2) education, skills or attitudes conducive to acquisition of further education and skills.

The main link between the household and the economy is the value of human time. The increased value of human time results in fewer children per household, with each child embodying greater investments in human capital. This, in turn, results in greater productivity in the economically active years. But this greater productivity further raises both the value of the unit of time and of income in the subsequent generation. Thus, over time the model predicts declining rates of population growth (zero rates or even negative rates for a time) and declining rates of infant mortality. Thus it appears that these economic trends are achieving what the zero population advocates have been urging. If so, dire predictions that the earth's resources will soon be used up are exaggerations.

From the standpoint of the central focus of this book, the Nerlove paper suggests that at least one organization, the family, is perhaps diminishing in size. A further implication is that the family is less a center of individual activity than it was previously. The greater education of the children and their parents leads to greater mobility and hopefully to a greater ability to deal with the increased complexities of modern urban industrial society. A positive and favorable note is that the increased value of time will lead to lower population growth. Lower population growth and greater productivity of individual family members provide some offset to the unfavorable developments that society has been experiencing resulting from the finite size of spaceship earth.

The first two essays of the book are wide ranging and are intended to provide background on the more focused subjects that are next treated. They have demonstrated that the framework for analyzing organizations and economic trends is necessarily broad, and that many different types of relationships are involved. Hopefully with the breadth of the background provided in these first two essays, the more acrimonious issues connected with the role of the large corporation can be viewed in a calmer and more objective framework.

ONE

Evaluating Organizations

Oscar Grusky

Professor of Sociology, UCLA

Dr. Oscar Grusky is chairman, Department of Sociology, University of California, Los Angeles. Education: Union College, Schenectady, New York, A.B., June, 1953; University of Michigan, Ann Arbor, Michigan, M.A. (Sociology), August, 1954; University of Michigan, Ann Arbor, Michigan, Ph.D. (Social Psychology), 1958.

Teaching Positions: University of Michigan, 1955-1957; University of Stockholm, Sweden, 1970-71; Department of Sociology, University of California, Los Angeles, 1957 to present.

Research Positions: principal investigator, National Science Foundation Project GS-186, "Experimental Studies of Succession and Effectiveness," 1962-66; principal investigator, Air Force Office of Scientific Research Project 769-65, "The Political Behavior of Military Elites," 1964-66; principal investigator, "Comparative Analysis of Military Career Patterns," Air Force Office of Scientific Research Project 1166-66, 1966-69; principal investigator, "Comparative Analysis of Military Career Patterns," project supported by Chancellor's Committee on International and Comparative Studies, Ford Foundation, UCLA, 1966-67; research specialist, Department of Mental Hygiene, State of California, 1970-71.

Consultant Positions: Psychological Clinic, University of Michigan, 1954-56; National Science Foundation, 1964 to present; Social Psychology Panel, State of California, Pacific State Hospital, 1965-67; Center for Sociocultural Research on Mental Disorder, Department of Mental Hygiene, State of California 1969-70; *American Journal of Sociology*, 1964-72; editorial consultant, *Sociometry*, 1962-65; associate editor, *Pacific Sociological Review*, 1965-68.

Among his publications are "Organizational Goals and the Behavior of Informal Leaders," *The American Journal of Sociology*, LXV, 1 (July 1959) 59-67; "Administrative Succession in Formal Organization," *Social Forces*, 39, 2 (December 1960), 105-115, reprinted in A. Gouldner and H. P. Gouldner, *Modern Sociology* (N.Y.: Harcourt, Brace & World, 1963), 389-396; "Corporate Size, Bureaucratization, and Managerial Succession," *The American Journal of Sociology*, LXVII, 3 (November 1961), 261-269, to be reprinted in Frank Baker (ed.) *Organizations, Individuals, and Health* (London: Tavistock Pub.); "Authoritarianism and Effective Indoctrination: A Case Study," *Administrative Science Quarterly*, 7, 1 (June 1962), 79-95, reprinted in *Personality and Social Systems*, 2nd ed., edited by N. J. Smelser and W. T. Smelser, (N.Y.: John Wiley and Sons, 1970), 636-646; "Managerial Succession and Organizational Effectiveness," *The American Journal of Sociology*, LXIX, 1 (July 1963), 21-31, reprinted in M. Straus and J. Nelson, *Sociological Analysis: An Empirical Approach Through Replication* (N.Y.: Harper and Row, 1968), P. Orleans (ed.), *Social Structure and Social Process* (With L. Churchill), "The Experimental Study of Organizational Variables," in O. Grusky and G. A. Miller (eds.) *The Sociology of Organizations: Basic Studies* (N.Y.: The Free Press, 1970).

My purpose is to discuss some of the problems involved in the evaluation of organizational functioning. The general theme of this book is "Large-Scale Enterprise in a Changing Society," but I do not intend to restrict my comments to business organizations alone. Quite the contrary, it is a central purpose of social science to develop generalizations that elicit understanding of the commonalities of all organized entities. Although business systems have certain special properties, they also possess features that characterize all complex organizations. My aim will be partially to sort out by comparative analysis the unique elements on the one hand, and the commonalities, on the other.

Everyone is interested in evaluating organizations. But why listen to a sociologist? Unlike professions like psychology, which has a strong component group of clinical psychologists, sociology is fundamentally an academically based group. The *National Science Register* for 1968 revealed that almost nine out of ten (88 percent) Ph.D.s in sociology were located in academic institutions. The comparable percentage for psychologists was only 60 percent. What does it mean to be academically based? I believe it means two main things:

First, the dominant orientation of sociologists is to the university and profession—which in its most positive light means that sociological research hopefully focuses first of all on scholarship and is typically not aligned to any particular applied orientation. Janowitz (1972) presents this example: "At a 1971 conference on community organization, a militant black community leader requested a well-known white sociologist to undertake a piece of research which would evaluate the effectiveness of an experimental education program in which he was deeply involved. When the sociologist raised the question of research access, the black community leader indicated that he felt such problems could be overcome by tact and patience, but he insisted that the result of the study would have to be submitted to a professional journal for publication. As an explanation, he indicated that 'if I go out and hire a commercial research organization—white or black—to work on a black community problem, they will very likely give me answers they think I want to hear. Only if I get your professional self-interest involved will I know that the results are worthwhile; and if you are going to publish them, I know they will be good and that you will not run out when the heat gets turned on.' "

Second, it means that the dominant client for the sociologist is the student and the professional and therefore that the sociologist's direct participation in public policy-making is likely to be considerably less strong than that of the economist or the psychologist. Boiled down to its essentials, I am arguing that sociologists might be worth listening to in part *because* they do not have to please their commercial client. I must, in candor, mention a counterargument—perhaps they are not often employed by business both because they may have little of industrial and practical use to offer, and because there may exist value differences centering around the appropriate role of government in dealing with social problems. Since sociology is the study of society and its preeminent purpose is reliable knowledge about our social work, and since such knowledge is of obvious concern to all, a sharing of ideas between business and social science should be mutually beneficial.

Our modern life takes place within the confines of complex organizations. Most infants are born in hospitals, whose bureaucratic routines determine how often and even what they are fed. After what has become a steadily increasing period of time with their parents, they enter school—first nursery school, then kindergarten, elementary, junior high, and high school. Their daily requirements are met by supermarkets, churches, department stores, and large restaurant chains. Upon graduation or perhaps before, the student goes to work, often for a large corporation, or chooses military service, or enters a highly bureaucratized university. If he opts for college, when he graduates he enters the work force and participates in big government, business, unions, or university organization. If he is taken ill, it is back to the large hospital, and when he eventually retires he may be off to Leisure World, a large housing development. When he is dead and buried by Forest Lawn, a large mortuary, his beneficiaries will rush off to a large insurance company to collect on his policy.

In such an organizational environment it behooves us to learn as much as possible about the impact of these complex systems on their members. One of the sociologist's tasks is to be skeptical and to question present wisdom. For example, it has often been asserted that bureaucracy produces conformity, indifference to human needs, lack of initiative, and an undue focus on red tape and deferral of decisions to superiors. "Calucci's Department" on television has depicted many of these sometimes laughable elements. A sociologist by the name of Kohn (1971) studied this problem and found in a cross-sectional study of 3,101 employed males in the United States striking evidence for the *opposite* view. Men who worked in bureaucratic organizations were more flexible intellectually, more open to new experiences, and self-directed in their values than were those who worked in nonbureaucratic organizations. I cite this study not only because it is illustrative of what I consider an appropriately skeptical perspective for the sociologist, but also because of its rigorous approach to the problem. Both characteristics are essential to the evaluative process. It should be remembered that there are a number of other equally valid ways of examining organizational phenomena in addition to a sociological or social science perspective, such as theology, fiction, poetry, drama, and philosophy.

1. WHAT IS EVALUATION?

Evaluation refers to the general process of appraisal, the means by which the value of a person, thing, or organization is ascertained. This process of assessment is basic to all social behavior. Evaluative research refers to the application of scientific techniques to the process of assessment (Schuman, 1967). Organizational evaluation refers to this process as it applies to persons and programs associated with formal organizations and with organizations as a whole. Evaluation is above all else a social and interactive process. It takes place within and between organizations. All organizations of necessity evaluate their members, other persons, and often other organizations. They do this primarily as a means of controlling their environment. An organization is a social system designed to generate a particular type or set of various types of outputs (Katz and Kahn, 1966). These outputs are dynamic and change as a product of both internal and environmental influences.

In order to produce outputs, an automobile, an educated student, or a rehabilitated addict, a social structure must be established. This structure, Max Weber (1947) has argued, necessitates that orders be transmitted through a chain of command, that is, a hierarchy is established with higher levels responsible for controlling and evaluating lower ones. The exercise of authority also takes place through detailed rules and memoranda that define expectations of behavior for members of the organization.

Barnard (1938) and later Gouldner (1954) have succeeded in showing that a serious limitation of Weber's approach lies in its one-way character. Control is in fact an interactive process between controlled and controller, so that subordinates are at times able to avoid undesirable rules and procedures. Hence, in place of the traditional approach that has examined the supervisor's effects on the worker, an alternative view has slowly developed that views the influence process as a reciprocal one. Lowin and Craig (1968) have recently shown experimentally that worker performance itself shapes closeness of supervision, initiating structure, and the degree of consideration the superior shows for the subordinate. Control is a general process through which organizations seek to induce their members to conform to their requirements (Tannenbaum, 1968). Evaluation is one aspect of control and refers to the process by which a member's performance or a unit's performance is compared with alternative standards. By way of contrasting control and evaluation, assembly-line production or interaction may be means of controlling workers' behavior, but they are not in themselves evaluation mechanisms.

2. DIMENSIONS OF THE EVALUATIVE PROCESS

Evaluation is an endemic process in postindustrial society. It characterizes families as well as organizations. It is an aspect of human interaction that is extremely important because it involves characterizing the object of evaluation in terms of his or her possibilites. Yet not all evaluation is the same, and one may differentiate among interpersonal, intraorganization, and interorganizational evaluations. A person may evaluate another person, as when one passer-by evaluates another on a sidewalk. Or a person may evaluate an organization, as when a candidate for a position assesses the firm which has offered him a job. Likewise, an organization evaluates a candidate before making him an offer. More precisely, a person acting for the organization evaluated the candidate. But a person as a representative of an organization is different from a person who acts independently.

Finally, an organization may evaluate another organization. This latter, or interorganizational evaluation, involves one or more persons acting for an organization in its assessments of another organization. The attributes of persons who work for or represent organizations often become attributes of the organization as a whole. As you know, organization members sometimes develop distinctive characteristics. Whether or not these characteristics are in the eyes of the beholder, evaluations between organizations inevitably involve some attribution of characteristics from persons to organizations.

Since organizations often have multiple objectives, a key area of disagreement is likely to center on the relative emphasis in the organization with regard to the set of goals it represents (Sills, 1957).

Both interpersonal and interorganizational evaluations may be distinguished along several dimensions. Evaluation may be personal or impersonal. Several organization theorists, but especially Blau and Scott (1962), have compared evaluation based on direct, personal relationships with that based on impersonal devices such as files and output records. Of course, both devices are likely to be used in organizations and hence the difference is partially in degree. Nevertheless, it is fundamentally different to be evaluated on the basis of observations associated with perceived personal attributes, such as friendliness, warmth, aggressiveness, and so on, as contrasted with output dimensions such as productivity. Although to some extent all evaluation may be based on perception of traits, there is generally an attempt to avoid such judgments officially. Hence, statistical records of output are utilized. Such records serve several purposes. First, they screen the superior and thereby dampen potential hostility toward him on the part of the subordinate. The supervisor can justify the decision not to promote a subordinate on "objective" grounds (Gouldner, 1954). Second, they enable the subordinate to more easily accept the manager's claims without submitting to him personally. Statistical records are applied generally across the board to all subordinates and hence are more difficult to disallow.

The same observations apply to evaluations between organizations. The Department of Health, Education, and Welfare now requires that Affirmative Action Programs be established in universitites receiving funds from the federal government. Compliance is based to a considerable extent on statistical records of changes in hiring policies with regard to employment of minorities and women.

Another dimension is frequency of evaluation. Persons, departments, or organizations may be evaluated occasionally, very often, or not at all. In general. the more frequently one is evaluated, the less autonomy one has, as Jacques (1956) has observed. Frequent supervision has been shown to generate considerable animosity (Day and Hamblin, 1964).

Some tasks are more prone to public evaluation than others. Consider, for example, the movie or television performer, the musician, or the professional football or baseball player, as compared with the public school teacher and the store clerk.

3. BASES OF INTERORGANIZATIONAL EVALUATION

Organizations evaluate one another not only because it has become normatively appropriate for them to do so, but also because in a competitive framework it is essential. Organizations exist in an environment of other organizations and establish relationships with these systems as a means of fulfilling their own functions.

One major basis of a relationship between organizations is *expertise.* A business firm will hire a management consulting firm, or an advertising agency, or a law firm, or accounting firm, simply because it feels that it can use the knowlege or expertness.

A second basis, related to the first, is *respect.* In this case the organization may simply try to model itself after another because of its high level of identification with that organization. Major business firms like IBM, GM, or universities such as Harvard find that other organizations frequently adopt practices they have established.

Third, evaluating organizations, as in the case of the HEW requirement concerning Affirmative Action Programs I noted, sometimes have the ability to withhold rewards if their evaluations are not accepted. French and Raven (1957) call this *coercive* power. The Internal Revenue Service and the FCC among other regulatory agencies hold this influence over many organizations. For example, the crucial evaluating organization for the radio and television industry is the Federal Communications Commission, which was established under the Communications Act of 1934. The FCC issues, reviews, and renews licenses for broadcasting and specifies the broadcaster's frequency, power, and other aspects of transmission. Naturally, such evaluations can be crucial.

Organizations such as the police, the courts, and the FBI have legitimate rights to prescribe certain behavior for organizations. Organizations thus exist in an environment of other interacting organizations. Interacting organizations develop agreement about the legitimacy of each other's activities in a particular field. This has been called "domain consensus" (Aldrich, 1972; Levine and White, 1961). It is alleged that where domain consensus exists interorganizational relationships will be cooperative rather than competitive.

From the above we can see that evaluating organizations may usefully be broken down into those legally mandated to evaluate the activities of other organizations, such as the courts, regulatary agencies such as the Federal Trade Commission, Civil Aeronautics Administration, public utilities commissions, the General Accounting Office of the federal government, legislative bodies, the attorneys general, police agenices, legally mandated consumer organizations, the Internal Revenue Service, and the like, on the one hand, and those organizations whose activities involve to a considerable extent evaluation of other organizations, but without a legal obligation to do so. The latter group would include Nader's Raiders, magazines such as *Fortune,* newspapers, and in fact much of the mass media, trade and professional organizations, such as the American Bar Association, and similar organizations. In the late 1960s we had an interesting example of an evaluating organization, the Federal Trade Commission, itself evaluated by Nader's Raiders in 1969 and then shortly thereafter as a product of these criticisms, evaluated again, this time by a committee of the American Bar Association created at the request of former

President Nixon. Both studies were highly critical of this agency. In this case, as is typical, the primary issue on which evaluation focused was organizational effectiveness.

4. EVALUATING ORGANIZATIONAL EFFECTIVENESS

Although effectiveness is crucial to the evaluation process, organization theorists have not been in agreement as to its meaning. Yuchtman and Seashore (1967), applying a systems approach, have defined organizational effectivenss as the "ability of the organization in either relative or absolute terms to exploit its environment in the acquisition of scarce and valued resources." And they continue that an organization is most effective when it "maximizes its bargaining position and optimizes its resource procurement." A very free translation of this is that an organization is effective if it is not only getting what it needs to function well but is also saving resources so that it can adapt to possible uneven times it may face in the future. *A major point omitted in this definition but which must be emphasized is that effectiveness depends on the criteria applied, and this in turn depends in part on the group affiliation and ideology of the evaluator.*

A central problem is formulating specific criteria of how well an organization is doing at a particular moment in time (Gross, 1964; Katz and Kahn, 1966). The following five criteria are applicable to all kinds of organizations:

(1) Output Indicators
(2) Satisfaction Indicators
(3) Throughput Indicators
(4) Adaptation Indicators
(5) Leadership Indicators

There is no intent to rank these five here. Each one contains numerous possible indicators. (1) Output refers to the products of the organization, which of course may be things, people, or both. Most frequently business firms produce objects, like MacDonald's hamburgers, while universities produce persons who ostensibly have learned as a result of their experiences in the organization. Nevertheless, some business firms achieve reputations as places which are especially skilled at training executives. Organizations typically have many types of output, and therefore a problem in evaluation lies in evaluation of each of these types. Amount of output may be a primary measure of effectiveness, or it may be quality of output. An adequate evaluation considers the problem of various output types and tradeoffs between quantity and quality. Organizations differentially stress quality versus quantity.

(2) Satisfaction refers to the extent to which the relevant needs of persons in the organization are being met. There are many "relevant needs" and many types of members of an organization. Organizations are highly stratified and the requirements of persons at different levels, the top executives, middle managers, lower-level managers and supervisors, and workers vary. In addition to satisfying these immediate members of the organization, it is essential to evaluate the degree of satisfaction of the clients, those with whom the organizational members relate. And finally, since all organizations exist within society, the satisfaction of the public at large is increasingly relevant to the effectiveness of the organization.

(3) We turn next to what I have called throughput indicators. These simply refer to the effectiveness of the actions the organization takes in transforming the input or raw materials into the output, or final products. Efficiency or unit cost is a commonly used throughput indicator as is return on investment or profitability.

(4) Adaptation indicators deal with the ability of the organization to change as conditions within the organization and in the environment are altered. This involves an assessment of organizational planning and flexibility in shifting throughput or technique and output as needs change. It also involves a planning capability, that is, an ability to anticipate likely changes and, most crucial, develop reserves of resources.

(5) The final indicator is leadership. Conventional wisdom insists that leadership is *the* most critical element and that leadership ability is a trait which some persons have and some do not. Over twenty years of

social psychological research which sought to identify such traits has produced failure and finally abandonment of the quest (Gibb, 1969). In its place has developed a view that it is not personality traits that are crucial, but instead interaction between the characteristics of the person and the situation in the organization within which the leader exists.

Research suggests there are several common assumptions about organizational effectiveness that have the character of myths and ought to be laid to rest. These include:

(1) The assumption that organizations have a single objective and therefore that evaluation of accomplishment or failure are simple assessments.

(2) The assumption that the requirements of effective organization are specific, unambiguous, and consensually agreed upon.

(3) The assumption that an organization can itself fully determine its level of effectiveness.

The set of indicators, since they are applicable to all organizations, suggest that single purpose formal organizations are imaginary in complex society. The ordering of the indicators vary in their importance to an organization depending upon the type of organization involved and its particular circumstances. Evaluation of an organization is many-sided and depends ultimately as noted on the perspective, ideology, and commitment of the evaluator. Within an organization there exist numerous important groups (owners, executives, managers, first-line supervisors, workers, clients) whose viewpoints and needs differ. Most evaluations, since they function as mechanisms of control, are conducted by management and reflect management objectives. As the set of criteria suggests there are many other equally valid perspectives. To satisfy the requirements of one group, such as top executives, may mean an inability to meet the needs of another, such as middle management. One cannot expect automatic agreement as to the appropriate allocation of resources in an organization. The result is potential conflict between various groups within the organization as well as between the organization and other groups in the environment.

Outside evaluation of organizations by government, for example, and consumer groups is becoming increasingly common. An organization's effectiveness is to a considerable extent determined by environmental, that is, societal influences. A business firm, for example, may be affected greatly by a war and just as greatly by a return to peace.

It has frequently been claimed (Downs, 1967; Olson, 1973) that a fundamental difference between public and private organizations is that the former—the police, the university, the mental hospital—have such vaguely formulated goals that they rely on self-evaluations of effectiveness of one form or another, while the latter—meaning business firms—because they have an output that can be priced on the market, have by contrast a very well-defined goal. As differentiation of public and private sectors becomes less clear—consider oil or medicine—these differences, such as they are, must of necessity fade. Certain aspects of output will remain somewhat different, however. Industrial firms can count the number of items of output, e.g., cars they produce, and football club owners can count attendance and other income, or note their team standing. Contrast this measure of effectiveness with that of UCLA or the Los Angeles Police Department. No university that I know of has attempted to assess how much "education" it produces nor how much more would be produced if the organization functioned differently. Would a radical reorganization of UCLA produce better educated students and more important research? Likewise, no police department knows the full extent of crime in the community or how major changes in the department's structure would affect its reduction. It is primarily through citizen reports that crimes become known to the police and citizens do not report all crimes—especially rapes, robberies, and assaults. According to the President's Commission on Law Enforcement and Administration of Justice, approximately 40 to 60 percent of all thefts and malicious mischief were unreported. (Victims indicated their failure to report was due to their feeling that police could or would not do anything.)

The usual outcome measures applied to educational organizations are number of graduates, dropout or transfer rate, student grade-point averages, achievement of graduate scholarships or higher degrees. These are not unimportant measures, but they do focus on what some

see as the fundamental objectives of a liberal education—one's capacity
for critical analysis, one's ability to reason carefully and intelligently,
and one's ability to enjoy a full and productive life. As Trow (1971)
puts it:

> Liberal education is in large part a substantial value in and of
> itself; it *is* the practices and relationships and patterns of behavior
> that enter into it, at least as much as it is some nebulous "out-
> come," difficult, if not impossible to measure, and showing itself
> in the whole life of the student after he leaves college.

Evaluations of higher educational organizations in these fundamental
terms are rare, but they are not impossible of attainment. Methods of
evaluation, employing longitudinal designs that would, for example,
follow a cohort systematically over a period of decades, are available
(Etzioni and Lehman, 1967). Organizations, private and public, tend
to rely overly much on quantitative rather than on qualitative indicators. UCLA is more likely to focus on the number of students it
instructs because such a figure is available and demanded, yet it says
little about the quality of its human output. Such evaluations are
clearly complex. Auto companies once used simple measures of
numbers of cars produced as a prime effectiveness measure. The large
number of defects led to a change whereby plant effectiveness now
includes not only raw amount and production cost but consideration of
the number of cars sent back for adjustment. Universities might
consider a comparable quality control program. Yet, to do so might
encourage some to seek to restrict the quality of input, and the eventual
result might be a highly elitist student body.

Corporation management programs tend to operate in like fashion.
Campbell *et al.* (1970) in their extensive research on business firms
noted the general feeling among business managers that the primary
reported definition of managerial success is "getting results." What is
meant by getting results is not always clear, but essentially it means
focusing on outcomes the company values, such as meeting output or
production quotas. The fundamental ethical problem resulting from
an emphasis on getting results is that accountability for *means* tends to
fall by the wayside. In general, considering the five types of effective-

ness indicators described, organizations favor most of all output, throughput, and adaptation measures, and have only recently, with greater affluence, looked with interest at the problem of satisfaction. Leadership indicators when considered have tended to be subjectively and unsystematically examined.

5. EVALUATING LEADERSHIP AND EFFECTIVENESS

A crucial dimension, at least as far as much social psychological theory is concerned as well as in the public mind, is the role of leadership in the effective functioning of organizations. Evaluating organizations often expend considerable effort in attempting to assess the relative effectiveness of the organization's leaders. For example, it is not uncommon that before investing large funds in stock purchases information on the firm's leadership capabilities will be sought by the investing organization. It is thus assumed that leadership accounts for a significant proportion of the variance with regard to the key outputs of the system in question. Yet, Lieberson and O'Connor (1972) in a detailed analysis of 167 large corporations found that very little of the variance in three performances measures—sales, earnings, and profit margins—could be explained by their leadership measure. Likewise, Butterfield (1968) found that leadership failed to predict effectiveness of branches of the Office of Administration of the National Aeronautics and Space Administration.

On the other hand, common sense leads us to believe that it makes a great deal of difference who is the president of the United States, the president of the corporation for which we work, the chancellor of the university, or the head coach of the Los Angeles Rams. In support of this common-sense view we have the recent research of Mott (1972), who has shown that how a leader acts makes a great deal of difference with regard to how his subordinates perceived his effectiveness. The greater the leader's anxiety, the less effective he was perceived to be. The issue should not be whether or not leadership affects organizational functioning but rather the conditions under which leadership accounts for or fails to account for a substantial proportion of the variance of effectiveness. Hence, we assume that *under certain circumstances* leadership may be irrelevant, whereas under others it would be crucial.

We would expect leadership to make more of a difference in effectiveness the higher the level the leader is in the organization and the freer the organization is of environmental control. The higher the level, the greater the executive's control over the system's resources; and the less the environmental constraints over the organization's functioning, the more the leader's actions affect the system's survival. Hence, environmental and situational constraints are crucial to any balanced theory of leadership behavior. One must be especially cautious in dealing with what have become very fuzzy concepts, leadership and effectiveness, for much too often they have been used as indicators of another. Baseball managers and football coaches know this well, for they have been its victims. If a team has a bad season, the manager is fired, and if they do exceptionally well, he becomes manager of the year (Grusky, 1963). The fallacy here is to use effectiveness as an *index* of leadership ability. This begs the question of how much variance leadership contributes to effectiveness by assuming automatically that it contributes a great deal.

We were able to demonstrate the strong impact of organizational effectiveness on a leader's view of himself and others' view of him in a seris of laboratory studies (Grusky, 1969, 1973; Grusky and Churchill, 1970). Seventy-two simulated business organizations were established in the laboratory and their effectiveness manipulated. After learning his role obligations in his first assignment, the manager (leader) was transferred to a new, identical organization which had a past history of high or low effectiveness under the predecessor's administration. The effectiveness of the organization under the new manager was then manipulated. Even though nothing the manager did actually influenced the effectiveness of the organization, we found that the leader's view of himself as a competent leader and the view of him by his immediate subordinates in the same terms was strongly linked by fluctuations in the effectiveness of the organization he led. Most importantly, this finding was independent of any previous leadership ability of the manager. The elimination of ability as a causal factor in a field study or field experiment would be exceedingly difficult, if not impossible. Hence, one of the distinct advantages of the experimental method employed was that it permitted examination of the effects of organizational effectiveness on leader self-image independent of the possibly contaminating influence of actual managerial ability or other personality traits.

Fiedler (1971) has also stressed that leader effectiveness is to a considerable extent situationally determined rather than simply a function of personality characteristics. Accordingly, he has proposed three major ways of improving leadership performance: "(a) training the leader to change his style, (b) assigning the leader to situations in which he will be effective, or (c) modifying the situation so that it will be appropriate to the leader's style or motivational pattern." Our findings related to the second way by suggesting that a leader's self-image would be significantly bolstered were the organization to become highly effective under his leadership *whether through his own efforts or not.* Also, the leader is more likely to be judged favorably by his subordinates if the organization under his predecessor had a past history of relative failure.

Much research in the past has stressed the presumed causal effects of the leader's performance on group effectiveness (Fiedler, 1967). An alternative approach is to view the leader as a victim of circumstances wherein the attribution of responsibility leads to a series of consequences for the organization and for the leader. It is not merely the performance of the leader but the *labeling of that performance by others* that appears to be decisive. Similarly, Graen, Dansereau, and Minami (1972) noted: "In conclusion, we believe that leadership style does make a difference within organizations. This difference may be not so much in terms of what the leader does but may be in terms of how it is interpreted by its members" (p. 235). Fiedler's (1970) research has shown surprisingly that leadership experience does not correlate positively with leadership performance. Nevertheless, persons in high places still subscribe to the belief that such a relationship exists. Likewise, the fallacious belief the leader was mainly responsible for the performance of the organization he commanded apparently produced the results we have reported. Research is needed that specifies those organizational factors affecting the attribution of responsibility to leaders.

Sapolsky (1972) has provided useful data to show that an organization's reputation for effectiveness may be as important as reality. He studied the Special Projects Office of the United States Department of the Navy and particularly its development role with regard to Polaris which was under the Fleet Ballistics Program. The Special Projects Office gained an outstanding reputation for innovativeness because it came up with PERT (Program Evaluation and Review Technique), a computerized research and development planning, scheduling, and control technique. Although later careful evaluations of PERT showed it to be of questionable value, the Special Projects Office was able through wide dissemination of this technique to foster what Sapolsky described as a myth of organizational effectiveness. His data showed that this management technique had little to do with the effective development of Polaris.

In Sapolsky's words, "these techniques were either not applied on a significant scale in the operations of the Special Projects Office until after the successful test and deployment of the initial FMB submarines, or they were applied, but did not work, or they were applied and worked, but had a totally different purpose than that officially described. The existence of an integrated, uniquely effective management system was a myth originated by the Special Projects Office. The further removed it was from its source, the more embossed the myth tended to become." The combination of "whirling computers, brightly colored charts, and fast-talking public relations officers gave the Special Projects Office" the appearance of a truly effective management system. But only the appearance. Sapolsky showed that this reputation for effectiveness was manipulated so as to provide higher authorities with such an aura of leadership skill that they then could command the kind of control over resources they felt necessary to develop Polaris.

We have then a situation where a questionably effective management technique is packaged successfully, thereby giving the organization a solid reputation, which, in turn, enabled it to obtain the resources and autonomy necessary to function quite well. This study shows the potential importance for effectiveness of the prior attribution to the leaders of a high level of capability. Expectations of capability can be self-fulfilling prophecies which contribute to the actual effectiveness of organizations. Likewise, expectations of leadership incapability, such as distrust of the leader, may set in motion events, some of which may be ambiguous and unclear, but which are viewed as supporting a pessimistic prognosis, and this, in turn, contributes to the organization's decline.

6. CAN ORGANIZATIONS EVALUATE THEMSELVES?

If evaluation is so important, why don't organizations evaluate themselves? Or can they? The answer, I believe, is that they can, but only in an incomplete fashion. Generally such evaluation is done to suit top-management purposes, and the result therefore omits consideration of many if not most of the five sets of key indicators I have described (Wildavsky, 1972). Insofar as large organizations consist of many interest groups with differing perspectives, it behooves management to encourage greater participation in the governance and hence the evaluation of the system as a whole. No matter how careful an organization is in evaluating itself, it is bound to be self-justifying. Outside judgment, and I mean judgment outside the executive group itself as well as outside the organization proper, is inevitably going to provide a fuller perspective, especially if the outsiders are not beholden to management.

Outside evaluation may increase the likelihood that broad societal interests and values will be included in the evaluation and specifically that questions such as these will be addressed:

(1) To what extent are positions of all kinds of the organization available to all segments of the society, especially minorities and women?

(2) How much opportunity exists for all members of the organization for advancement and learning within the system?

(3) To what extent are members pleased with their work and

with themselves as persons as a product of the tasks they perform in the organization?

(4) To what extent can organization members and clientele influence those who make the major decisions that affect them in the organization?

Review of research concerning the effects of participation on decision-making suggests that if you involve the entire work group in a problem-solving or decision-making task rather than simply allow the manager to decide, the likelihood is that two desirable effects will be produced: (1) the decision is more likely to be accepted by the members, and (2) relatedly, the decision is more likely to be carried out to fruition in a more efficient fashion. On the other hand, to involve more persons in the decision process requires a considerably greater amount of man-hours of effort (Vroom, 1969). Yet, it would be naïve to argue that participation in decision-making tasks at all levels is uniformly desirable. Imagine the Los Angeles Rams trying to function in such fashion—they would face a succession of delay-of-the-game penalties. However, it is reasonable and consistent to claim that provision of adequate means for involvement in major task areas of an organization provides important and valuable human rewards and therefore ought to be encouraged even though available data are inconclusive as to the long-term effects of such increased participation on productivity.

The history of business organization is one of shifting control from the state, as in the Roman Empire, to the owner after the industrial revolution, to the present situation where power resides primarily in the professional manager and staff. Two groups have been noticeably omitted if not largely ignored in this development—the worker and the consumer-client. We can rather easily discover the architect and the construction firm that built this auditorium, but the workers whose sweat intermingled with the bricks that were laid and the I-beams that were swung, are now unknown and forgotten. The workers do have unions and hence some representation of their interests, but it would be folly to assume their control approximates that of business. Even where unions exist, the workers' participation in the ongoing decision-making activities of the organization is minor, as unions are of course themselves large, bureaucratic structures. The consumer or client in service organizations is another typically underrepresented group. The weakest and least organized group in the economic sphere is still the consumer; in health-care organizations it is the patient; and in education, the student. No democratic society has yet succeeded in effectively including worker and consumer-client interests in the conduct of its business firms (Liebhafsky, 1971), its health-care system (Alford, 1972), its criminal justice system (Ohlin, 1973), or its educational institutions (Jencks and Riesman, 1969). The development of organizations that strive to accomplish this aim is the proper role of evaluation.

Evaluation and social control are intimately linked. Organizations evaluate their operations and are themselves evaluated by other organizations largely because their environment is characterized by uncertainty (Thompson, 1967). The evaluation process functions to provide information that may enable the organization to better influence and control its environment. Evaluation, in short, can help join knowledge with power. Active participation in society generates organization which in turn accelerates the possibility of evaluation of prevailing practices in organizations. Likewise, knowledge of *different* possibilities encourages truly critical evaluation.

REFERENCES

Aldrich, Howard E. "Technology and Organizational Structure: A Reexamination of the Findings of the Aston Group." *Administrative Science Quarterly*, XVII, 1 (1972), 26-43.

Alford, Robert R. "The Political Economy of Health Care: Dynamics Without Change." Andover, Mass.: Warner Module Publications, Inc., 1972 (R96).

Barnard, Chester I. *The Functions of the Executive*, Cambridge, Mass.: Harvard University Press, 1938.

Blau, Peter M., and W. Richard Scott. *Formal Organizations*. San Francisco: Chandler, 1962.

Butterfield, D. A. "An Integrative Approach to the Study of Leadership Effectiveness in Organizations." Ph.D. thesis, University of Michigan. 1968.

Campbell, John P., Marvin D. Dunnette, Edward E. Lawler III, and Karl E. Weick, Jr. *Managerial Behavior, Performance, and Effectiveness.* New York: McGraw-Hill, 1970.

Coleman, James. "Loss of Power." *American Sociological Review,* 38, 1 (1973), 1-17.

Day, Robert C., and Robert L. Hamblin. "Some Effects of Close and Punitive Styles of Supervision." *The American Journal of Sociology* (1964), 499-510.

Downs, Anthony. *Inside Bureaucracy.* Boston, Mass.: Little, Brown & Co., 1967.

Etzioni, Amitai and Edward W. Lehman. "Some Dangers in 'Valid' Social Measurement." *The Annals of the Amer. Acad. of Political and Social Science,* 373 (1967), 1-15.

Fiedler, Fred E. *A Theory of Leadership Effectiveness.* New York: McGraw-Hill, 1967.

———. "Leadership Experience and Leader Performance—Another Hypothesis Shot to Hell." *Organizational Behavior and Human Performance,* 5 (1970), 1-14.

French, John R. P., Jr., and Bertram Raven. "The Bases of Social Power" in D. Cartwright (ed.), *Studies in Social Power.* Ann Arbor, Mich. Institute for Social Research.

Gibb, Cecil. "Leadership." In Gardner Lindsey and Elliot Aronson (eds.), *The Handbook of Social Psychology.* Reading, Mass.: The Addison-Wesley Publishing Co., 1969.

Gouldner, Alvin W. *Patterns of Industrial Bureaucracy.* New York: The Free Press, 1954.

Graen, George, Fred Dansereau Jr., and Takao Minami. "Dysfunctional Leadership Styles." *Organizational Behavior and Human Performance,* 7 (1972), 216-236.

Gross, Bertram M. *The Managing of Organizations.* 2 vols. New York: The Free Press, 1968.

Grusky, Oscar. "Managerial Succession and Organizational Effectiveness." *The American Journal of Sociology,* LXIX, 1 (1963), 21-31.

———. "Succession with an Ally." *Administrative Science Quarterly* 14, 2 (June 1969), 155-170.

———. "An Experiment on the Effects of Organizational Effectiveness on Leader Self-Image." Unpublished paper.

Grusky, Oscar, and Churchill Lindsey. "The Experimental Study of Organizational Variables." in O. Grusky and G. A. Miller (eds.), *The*

Sociology of Organizations: Basic Studies. New York: The Free Press,˙1970.

Hardin, Garret. "The Tragedy of the Commons." *Science,* 1962 (1968), 1243-1248.

Jacques, Eliot. *Measurement of Responsibility.* London: Tavistock Publications, 1956.

Janovitz, Morris. "Professionalization of Sociology." *The American Journal of Sociology,* 78, 1 (1972), 105-135.

Jencks, Christopher, and David Riesman. *The Academic Revolution.* Garden City, New York: Anchor, 1969.

Katz, Daniel, and Robert L. Kahn. *The Social Psychology of Organizations.* New York: John Wiley and Sons, 1969.

Kohn, Melvin. "Bureaucratic Man: A Portrait and An Interpretation." *American Sociological Review,* 36, 3 (1971), 461-474.

Levine, Sol, and Paul E. White. "Exchange as a Conceptual Framework for the Study of Interorganizational Relationships." *Administrative Science Quarterly,* 5 (1961), 583-601.

Lieberson, Stanley, and James F. O'Connor. "Leadership and Organizational Performance: A Study of Large Corporations." *American Sociological Review,* 37, 2 (1972), 117-130.

Liebhafsky, H. H. *American Government and Business.* New York: John Wiley and Sons, 1971.

Lowin, Aaron, and James R. Craig. "The Influence of Level of Performance on Managerial Style: An Experimental Object-Lesson in the Ambiguity of Correlational Data." *Organizational Behavior and Human Performance,* 3 (1968), 440-458.

Mott, Paul. *The Characteristics of Effective Organizations.* New York: Harper & Row, 1972.

Ohlin, Lloyd E. *Prisoners in America.* Englewood Cliffs, N.J.: Prentice-Hall, Inc., 1973.

Olson, Mancur. "Public Services on the Assembly Line." *Evaluation,* 1, 2 (1973), 37-41.

Sapolsky, Harvey. *The Polaris System Development.* Cambridge, Mass.: Harvard University Press, 1972.

Sills, David L. *The Volunteers.* Glencoe, Ill.: The Free Press, 1957.

Suchman, Edward A. *Evaluative Research.* New York: Russell Sage Foundation, 1967.

Tannenbaum, Arnold S. *Control in Organizations.* New York: McGraw-Hill, 1968.

Thompson, James D. *Organization in Action.* New York: McGraw-Hill, 1967.

Trow, Martin. "Methodological Problems in the Evaluation of Innovation." In Frances Caro (ed.), *Readings in Evaluation Research.* New York: Russell Sage Foundation, 1971.

Vroom, Victor. "Industrial Social Psychology." In Gardner Lindsey and Elliot Aronson (eds.), *The Handbook of Social Psychology.* Reading, Mass.: The Addison-Wesley Publishing Co., 1969.

Weber, Max. *The Theory of Social and Economic Organizations.* Translated by A. M. Henderson and Talcott Parsons and edited by Talcott Parsons. Glencoe, Ill.: The Free Press, 1947.

Wildavsky, Aaron. "The Self-Evaluating Organization." *Public Administration Review* (September/October 1972), 509-520.

Yuchtman, Ephrain and Stanley E. Seashore. "A System Resource Approach to Organizational Effectiveness." *American Sociological Review,* 32, 6 (1967), 841-903.

TWO

Household and Economy: Toward

a New Theory of Population

and Economic Growth *

Marc Nerlove

Professor of Economics
University of Chicago

Previous and Present Positions: analytical statistician, U.S. Department of Agriculture, 1956-57; first lieutenant, U.S. Army, 1957-59; economist Subcommittee on Antitrust and Monopoly, U.S. Senate, 1958; visiting lecturer in political economy, John Hopkins, 1958-59; associate professor of economics and agricultural economics, University of Minnesota, 1959-60; professor of economics, Stanford University, 1960-65; Fulbright and Guggenheim Fellow, Netherlands School

* I am indebted to Gary S. Becker, Glen Cain, Richard B. Freeman, Margaret G. Reid, and T. W. Schultz for discussions concerning the subject of this paper and for comments on a related paper. Virginia Thurner contributed valuable editorial advice.

of Economics, 1962-63; professor of economics, Yale University, 1965-69; Frank W. Taussig Research Professor of Economics, Harvard University, 1967-68; professor of economics, University of Chicago, 1969- ; consultant: the RAND Corporation (1959-); Visiting Cook Professor of Economics, Northwestern University, 1973-74.

Degrees: B.A. (Honors), 1952, University of Chicago; M.A., 1955, Ph.D. (Distinction), 1956, John Hopkins University; M.A. (Hon.), 1965, Yale University.

Affiliations: Phi Beta Kappa, American Economic Association, American Statistical Association, (Fellow), Econometric Society (Fellow; Council, 1962-68), Population Association, Royal Economic Society (Fellow), American Acadmey of Arts and Sciences (Fellow).

Publications: *Distributed Lags and Demand Analysis,* 1958; *The Dynamics of Supply: Estimation of Farmers' Response to Price,* 1958; *Estimation and Identification of Dobb-Douglas Production Functions,* 1965; *Studies in the Analysis of Economic Time Series,* with D. M. Grether and J. L. Carvalho, University of Chicago Press, forthcoming: more than fifty articles in professional journals, conference volumes, symposia and *Festschriften.*

It is somewhat unusual to begin the treatment of a subject with a warning against attaching too much importance to it; but in the case of economics, such an injunction is quite as much needed as explanation and emphasis of the importanance it really has. It is characteristic of the age in which we live to think too much in terms of economics, to see things too predominantly in their economic aspect. . . . There is no more important prerequisite to clear thinking in regard to economics itself than is recognition of its limited place among human interests at large. [FRANK H. KNIGHT, 1933 (1965)]

This research was supported by a grant from the Rockefeller Foundation to the University of Chicago for the study of the economics of population and family decision-making.

1. INTRODUCTION: MALTHUS REVISED

Malthus, in essays published in 1798 and 1830, and the classical economists combined a very simple model of family decision-making—procreation without bound except possibly by "a foresight of the difficulties attending the rearing of a family ... and the acutal distresses of some of the lower classes, by which they are disabled from giving the proper food and attention to their children" (Malthus, 1970, p. 89)—with an equally simple model of the operation of the economy. According to the latter, a high level of capital accumulation induced by a high level of profits—representing the difference between output and the rent of land (natural resources) and wages—permitted a continual increase in output and population, albeit at the cost of resort to land of increasingly poorer quality; it did not, as the result of the model of family decision-making, lead to a rising standard of living for most people. Thus, the classsical economists achieved a very simple model of economic growth and development (Baumol, 1970, pp. 13-21). Modern growth theorists in the tradition of Solow (1956) and Swan (1956) have developed theories of economic growth based on far more elaborate theories of the economy, but few theories of population growth and family decision-making have gone beyond the Malthusian model (Pitchford, 1973, pp. 1-10). Although natural-resource constraints may be readily incorporated through the device of diminishing returns to scale in the variable factors (Swan, 1956, pp. 340-42), it is a constant proportional rate of population growth, perhaps aided and abetted by exogenous technological progress, that essentially drives the mechanism. Discussions of the optimal rates of population growth or level of population do often attempt to integrate an endogenously determined population in the model. But none, to my knowledge, have examined the feedback from changes in the economy and changes in the relative prices and costs which families face when they decide how many children they will have and what they will invest in those children's health, nutrition, or education, although Pitchford (1973) does discuss the costs of and returns of population control at the macro level.

In recent years, the recognition, crucial to the understanding of long-term growth, that much investment which occurs in the economy is made in human beings rather than in physical capital and that fertility itself is shaped in important ways by economic considerations has led to renewed interest in the economics of the household decisions. In that type of unit, not only decisions about fertility, but also those related to investments in human capital, consumption and savings, migration, labor-force participation, and, in a sense, marriage itself, are made.

With this in mind, in Section 2 I briefly and critically describe the fundamental elements of the largely static theory of household production and choice. This theory was developed in its modern form by Gary Becker (1965) and others, but most of its essentials originated in the much earlier work of Margaret Reid (1934), and its owes a great deal to Wesley Mitchell's seminal observations in his essay (1912) on "The Backward Art of Spending Money." Section 3 concludes this paper with some speculations on how the "new home economics" may be integrated in a theory of economic growth and development through an understanding of the way in which investment in human capital increases the value of human time and thus changes over time the resource constraints and the relative costs and prices which "households" face in their decisions on the number and quality of children they attempt to produce. The question as to whether this constitutes a true economic explanation of the so-called demographic transition, and thus a revision of the Malthusian tradition, is basically an empirical one and is left open.

2. THE "NEW HOME ECONOMICS": SUMMARY AND CRITIQUE

In its most unadorned form, economics is the theory of allocation of limited resources among competing ends in order to maximize satisfactions (or utility), subject to the constraints imposed by limitations in the availability of the resources required to achieve those ends. Various elaborations and accretions are necessary to accommodate this central theoretical core to the dynamics of choices made sequentially over time and in the presence of uncertainty regarding future constraints and future preferences. At several points I shall have more to say about our present failure to reach successful accommodations in our underlying theory in these directions, as well as about our even more important limitations as economists to cope with the whole complex of issues raised by intergenerational transfers, within society as an ongoing concern, and particularly within the family.

The first element in the new home economics is the utility function to be maximized. Its form and its arguments (i.e., what variables determine its level) are obviously crucial in determining the choices which result from its maximization. But whose utility function is it that is maximized in connection with choices pertinent to marriage, children, consumption of commodities, work and leisure, and investment in all forms of capital? Considering the household as already formed, much of the theoretical underpinning rests on what I have called elsewhere the "Chicago model" (Nerlove, 1972*b*).[1]

The "Chicago utility function," if I may call it that, has several key characteristics. First, it does not involve nonmarket goods or physical commodities and purchasable services as we usually think of them in economics, but its arguments are abstract goods composed of a number of "attributes" which must themselves be produced within the household (Becker, 1965; Lancaster, 1966; Muth, 1966). The importance of this characteristic of the utility function is that it leads directly to the key questions of household technology and the composition of different types of market goods and services and physical commodities, in terms of attributes contributing to satisfactions. This, indeed, is the point made forcefully by Muth (1966) and recently emphasized by Michael and Becker (1972). Earlier (1947), Leontief pointed out that the theory of consumer behavior as then developed, although of great generality, lacked content to the extent that it gave no clue to the types of relations to be expected among different categories of goods.

The assumption of the existence of general categories of needs, different from demands for particular individual commodities, but still specific enough to be clearly distinguishable from each other, is basic to the man-in-the-street idea of consumers' demand.

One speaks of the desire for food as existing behind and separately from the particular demand for bread, apples, or Lobster à la Newburg. This need for food is at the same time spoken of as something clearly distinguishable from the similarly general needs for clothing or, say, for shelter, each of the latter also thought of as existing separately although manifested through the particular demands for one-family houses, apartment flats, or woolen suits and raincoats. [Leontief, 1947, p. 371]

Strotz (1957), in his introduction of the notion of a utility tree and in his later (1959) discussion with Gorman, attempted to give more empirical content to the theory of consumer demand in precisely this way, although he interpreted his results in terms of a "budgeting" process. An important aspect of the household-production model, including time and market-purchasable goods, as introduced by Becker (1965), Lancaster (1966), and Muth (1966), is precisely, as Muth points out, that it does yield "a utility function which is weakly separable when viewed as a function of commodities purchased on the market" (Muth, 1966, p. 700). While it is true, in a sense, that many conclusions of the "new home economics" could be derived directly from Strotzian utility trees and other specializing assumptions, the home-production aspect of the Chicago function lends an intuitive insight and empirical content which are lacking in the more abstract formulation. It suggests a more direct look at the technology of processes within the household and particularly at how such processes use household time and nonpurchased inputs in addition to market-purchasable commodities. Indeed, the supposed differences in the time intensity of the production of household goods give much of the content to recent applications of the "new home economics" to the problems of fertility and human capital formation.[2] I return to this point in Section 3 where I speculate on how the increasing value of human time works through a Chicago utility function/household-production model to alter the behavior of generations through time.

A second key characteristic of the Chicago utility function is that it is just that: one utility function—the welfare of the children and other members of the family is assumed to enter the utility function of a single decision-maker (not always the husband and father!), thus obviating the assumption of a "family utility function" with all the concomitant problems of social utility functions in general. It is perhaps not entirely accurate to identity this position too closely with Chicago; it should perhaps be called "Samuelsonian finesse." Samuelson (1956) writes:

> Where the family is concerned the phenomenon of altruism inevitably raises its head: if we can speak at all of the indifference curves of any one member, we must admit that his tastes and marginal rates of contribution are contaminated by the goods that other members consume. These . . . external consumption effects are the essence of family life. . . . Such problems of home economics are, abstractly conceived, exactly of the same logical character as the general problem of government and social welfare. [p. 9]
> . . . if within the family there can be assumed to take place an optimal reallocation of income so as to keep each member's dollar expenditure of equal ethical worth, then there can be derived for the whole family a set of well-behaved indifference contours relating the totals of what it consumes: the family can be said to *act as if* it maximizes such a group preference function. [p. 21]

The problem with the Samuelsonian finesse, however, is that it assumes a fixed family membership, and a great deal of what the Chicago utility function is designed to explain is how that family composition gets determined. This requires much more than Samuelson allows for in his formulation. When, for example, are children members of the family, and thus codeterminers of the utility function, and when are they just arguments in the utility function determined for the family not including them? The full internalization argued by T. W. Schultz (1972*b*) seems a necessary addition to the argument. Yet, for this to be true, what might be called the "John Donne effect" must be extremely powerful. Casual observation suggests that each individual's concern for others diminishes with distance in both time and space. Yet it may be true under certain restrictive assumptions, as pointed out to me by Assaf Razin, that what might be called pairwise intergenerational internalization (by which I mean full internalization of the utilities of the next succeeding generation by the immediately preceding generation) would lead to essentially the same type of problem as that encountered in the discussions of optimal growth with an infinite horizon.

Morishima (1970, pp. 213-25) presents an extended discussion of some of the more technical issues involved in formulating dynamic utility functions and the conditions under which such functions can be reduced to the sum of discounted utilities of each future generation or at each future point in time, irrespective of the generation involved. In general, these conditions are highly restrictive and closely related to the conditions of Strotz (1959) and Gorman (1959) for strong separability of the utility function. But as Koopmans (1967, p. 96) points out, the problem is really in some sense an ethical one:

> What is at issue is clearly an intertemporal distribution problem: that of balancing the consumption levels of successive generations, and of successive stages in the life-cycle of a given cohort of contemporaries. The most pertinent decisions—individual, corporate, or governmental—are those that determine investment in physical capital, in human capital, and in research and development. Investments in physical capital, if well made, augment future consumption through an increase in future capital-labor ratios. Investment in human capital raises the quality of labor and, one hopes, of life. Successful research and development augment future capital and labor inputs through the development of better techniques of production.

Even regarded as a strictly behavioral model, pairwise internalization, which seems central to the Chicago utility function, has most important implications for the intergenerational transfers of material wealth and human capital which Knight (1921, pp. 374-75) has so eloquently described as central to the continuity of the social order.[3] Some of these implications bear on the issues discussed in the next section. Here, however, it seems essential to point out the profound problems in, on the one hand, internalizing all the family members' satisfactions in one utility function and, at the same time, using this same utility function to determine the number and "quality" of the family members themselves. Essentially the problem results from the condensation of a sequential, dynamic set of decisions into a theory of choice based on the maximization of a single, static, timeless utility function. In its most extreme form, the issue of the conceptual adequacy of the approach arises in connection with the application of the new home economics to household formation—a formation which in an earlier, less aberrant, and nonconformist era might have been described as "marriage"! Yet marriage, in some sense, remains very much associated with procreation; and the act of marriage, or at least of household formation, is the normal first step in the central process of choice with which the new home economics deals. Where then is the utility function? Can the entire process really be separated into two distinct parts, what the econometrician would call a recursive system? If a fundamental purpose of marriage is the procreation of a couple's own legitimate children, given a society's definition of both marriage and legitimacy, clearly the process cannot be regarded as recursive.[4] Again, the static character of the analysis, while not necessarily limiting its usefulness in an empirical sense, introduces a conceptual difficulty of a high order.

The second element in the new home economics is the technology of household production described by a production function or functions and a list of the resources utilized in the processes involved. Typically, following Becker (1965), the inputs are time, perhaps distinguishable by household member (e.g., husband and wife) and market-purchasable commodities. These inputs are used to produce within the household the goods and services that in turn lead to satisfaction. In the simplest form in the economic theory of fertility, two time inputs (the husband's and wife's) and one general market-purchasable commodity are assumed in the household technology to produce three household goods: child numbers, child quality, and a general commodity called "other satisfactions" (Willis, 1973; DeTray, 1973). In all analyses to date an important further simplification of this basic technological structure has been made: each good entering the utility function is assumed to be produced by a separate independent production process. Jointness in production arises not because of common overhead factors within the household, but because the factor inputs available to the household are subject to overall constraints.[5] Willis (1973) and DeTray (1973), for example, both assume that child quality per child and child numbers are produced by independent production processes. Each factor separately enters the household utility function in the Willis formulation.

The one is simply multiplied with the other to arrive at the final good, child services, which is assumed to enter the household utility function in DeTray's formulation. Both child numbers and child quality are generally assumed to be mother's time intensive.

The third element in the new home economics is a set of assumptions about the way in which household resources, principally time, can be transformed into market-purchasable commodities to be used in the household-production process. Strictly speaking, I suppose one could consider this set of assumptions as part of the general technology of household production and subsumed under the second element of the theory. It is, however, better to treat the matter separately, since most of what is involved concerns the terms upon which household members can enter the labor market, the wages they can earn, and, somewhat secondarily, the prices at which market commodities can be purchased. It is here that the lack of dynamic character of the new home economics cuts most deeply into its potential implications for the central problem of fertility and female labor-force participation. The timing and spacing of children, the opportunities for part-time work and accumulation of lifetime labor market experience, and choices as to the amount of education to be invested in early in the life cycle all revolve heavily on the terms under which women can participate in the labor market and thus share in the transformation of the household's time resources into market commodities. The human capital literature (Ben-Porath, 1967; Mincer, 1970, 1973) is, of course, replete with dynamic analyses of investment in human capital over time and the life-cycle effects of these investments on earnings. But little of this work has entered the more general framework of the "new home economics," particularly as this theory bears on decisions concerning the numbers of children and their timing and spacing within a marriage and the relation of these decisions to the accumulation of other forms of assets. The work of Heckman (1971), Ghez and Becker (1972), and an unpublished work of Frank Stafford does, however, represent a notable beginning of the extension of this part of theory into more dynamically relevant realms.[6] Yet we need to understand far more than we presently do about why the labor market functions so differently for men than for women, the role of institutional constraints, discrimination, and the relation of these to women's choices of occupation and timing of labor-force participation.

Once again, the simultaneities of the system severely limit our ability to break out a single segment for proper analysis.

The fourth and final element in the new home economics is the resource constraints facing the household in its production and optimization decisions. Traditionally these constraints are divided into time (husband's and wife's, although often the husband is assumed to devote full time to the market) and "other" nonwage income. While it is universally recognized that some elements of household production and consumption—sleep and food, for example—are in fact inputs into the production-of-time resources, little attention has thus far been paid to the quality of the time resources and of other family resources—both genetic and material—passed from one generation to the next. Arleen Leibowitz's study of Terman's 1921 sample of California school children bears importantly on the manner in which much human capital is passed from one generation to another, especially to a child of preschool age. The sample is very unrepresentative, but it is instructive, for the investments in her child of a mother's time and the quality of those investments, as measured by her education, are found to affect appreciably later measures of the child's ability and future earning capacity.

The resource constraints facing the household, once it is formed, are, of course, a product of the household formation itself and thus connected with my earlier remarks on the inseparability of this complex of issues, from those of family choice and decision-making. But, more important it is in this area that the complex issue of intergenerational transfers figures most prominently. We live, after all,

> in a world where individuals are born naked, destitute, helpless, ignorant, and untrained, and must spend a third of their lives in acquiring the prerequisites of a free contractual existence. . . . The fundamental fact about society as a going concern is that it is made up of individuals who are born and die and give place to others; and the fundamental fact about modern civilization is that it is dependent upon the utilization of three great accumulating funds of inheritance from the past, material goods and appliances, knowledge and skill, and morale. Besides the torch of life itself, the material wealth of the world, a technological system of vast and

increasing intricacy and the habituations which fit men for social
life must in some manner be carried forward to new individuals
born devoid of all these things as older individuals pass out. The
existing order, with the institutions of the private family and
private property (in self as well as goods), inheritance and bequest
and parental responsibility, affords one way for securing more or
less tolerable results in grappling with this problem. [Knight, 1921,
pp. 374-75]

So the apparently simple theoretical construct of a time budget plus
other income constraint to the household conceals beneath its serene
and mathematically differentiable exterior the central problem of the
continuity of society itself.[7]

By themselves the four main elements of the theoretical structure of
the new home economics—(1) a utility function with arguments which
are not physical commodities but home-produced bundles of
attributes; (2) a household production technology; (3) an external
labor-market environment providing the means for transforming
household resources into market commodities; and (4) a set of household resource constraints—are incapable of yielding a series of well-
defined implications about the main problems of household behavior
with which we are concerned. It is only a framework within which to
think about these problems. Many special additional assumptions,
some of which have been mentioned, must be added to the framework
to arrive at empirically refutable propositions. Moreover, the nature of
the required additional specifications is intimately related to the peculiarities of the particular bodies of data to which the new home
economics has been applied. These data range all the way from
aggregate time-series data covering long periods of time, to cross-sectional census data for both large and small geographic regions at a
point in time and over time, to household and family data based on
individual interviews, with and without collection of retrospective
information.

If to the key simplification involved in the assumption of separable
independent productive processes within the household, one adds the
assumptions that young children are highly intensive of the mother's
time in comparison with other activities within the home and older

children are less intensive, and that for institutional or biological reasons the comparative advantage of the male partner in the acquisition of market-purchasable commodities significantly exceeds that of the female partner, a number of interesting implications of the theory emerge which are tolerably well supported by the empirical evidence so far analyzed. Setting aside for the moment the inadequacy of the observed market wage to measure the cost of a nonworking woman's time, the immediate implication of the theory is that a rise in cost of mother's time for the family will cause a substitution away from time-intensive goods such as children and toward those requiring more inputs of market-purchasable commodities. Indeed, if we further assume momentarily that males are completely specialized in market activities, changes in their wages represent pure income effects for the family, and we do then observe for families with working mothers positive association of family size with income and negative association with female wage rates. To the extent that education serves as a proxy for the relative costs of time which may measure some of these costs less imperfectly, or at least in a fashion different from market wages, similar differences are observed between the effects of male and female educational attainments (Mincer, 1963; Nerlove and Schultz, 1970; Willis, 1973; DeTray, 1973; Ben-Porath, 1973).

Turning the analysis around, we can ask what implications the new home economics has for female labor-force participation. The new home economics predicts what is perhaps the obvious: the composition of a woman's family is strongly associated with her labor-force participation. Typically, the number of a family's children under the age of eighteen and the age of the youngest child are both strong predictors of a woman's labor-force participation. These facts about family composition have been interpreted by Cain (1966), for example, as measures of the opportunity value of a mother's time in the home. Gronau (1973) attempted a detailed and sophisticated analysis of just this proposition, using a subsample of the 1/1000 sample from 1960 United States Census; moreover, he examined the interaction of educational attainment with family composition. Others (Smith, 1972; Leibowitz, 1972) have documented that highly educated married women participate to a greater extent in the labor force and work more hours when they do work than married women with less schooling.

Married women as a group also tend to withdraw from the labor force when they have children; this is an implication of the new home economics, on the assumption that children are more female time intensive than other commodities produced within the home; but the rates at which women with different educational attainments withdraw is not the same. During the child-rearing years, more highly educated women reallocate more hours to household production than do women with less education. Ben-Porath's (1973) finding of a U-shaped relation between education and labor-force participation for Israeli women with young children strongly suggests differences in the effects of education at different levels on the relative efficiencies of home and market production and also interactions between female education and child quality. But all of this has been insufficiently explored within the presently existing framework of the new home economics. As Sweet (1968), Nerlove and Schultz (1970), and Hall (1973) have emphasized, educational investments, labor-force participation, and fertility must be viewed, at least partly, as simultaneously determined choices. This is surely one of the most important implications of the new home economics and only partly negated by the latter's currently static character.

Finally, if we regard, as I think we must, the grand problem of the new home economics as the explanation of the demographic transition, that is, the "economic and social processes and family behavior that accounts for the marked decline from very high birth and death rates to modern very low birth and death rates" (T. W. Schultz, 1973b, p. S4), the new home economics does have some insights, albeit limited, to offer (O'Hara, 1972). Clearly, a high probability of child mortality affects the costs of achieving a given family size, that is, the number of children surviving to a given age. If it is assumed that on the whole parents achieve a greater (discounted) sum of satisfactions the longer a child survives and if declines in mortality result in greater relative increases in the conditional probabilities of survival from earlier ages to successively older ages, declines in mortality should tend, according to the new home economics, to generate a greater demand for children. This need not lead to an increase in births, however, since such declines in mortality lower the cost of child quality relative to the cost of number of children. Of course, the net effect must depend on the technology of the production of child numbers and child quality as well as on the relative importance of these in the utility function. These factors, of course, may vary substantially from time to time, culture to culture, and place to place. The elucidation of such effects, however, must surely constitute one of the central challenges to the empirical application of the new home economics. To explore such effects fully, however, requires that the household decision-making process be accommodated in a model of economic growth and development, a subject to which we now turn.

3. HOUSEHOLD DECISION-MAKING AND ECONOMIC GROWTH: SPECULATIONS AND CONJECTURES

"Would you tell me, please, which way I ought to go from here?"
"That depends a good deal on where you want to go," said the Cat. [*Alice's Adventures in Wonderland*]

In his classic paper on "Diminishing Returns from Investment," Knight (1944) pointed out that "if new investment can be freely directed to all uses, i.e., embodied in all types of productive agents indifferently, it will not be subject to diminishing returns" (p. 33). Moreover, he stressed, as did Marshall before him, the concept of capital in human beings, and that "in the production of laborers the matter of 'quality' is far more important than that of quantity in the crude sense of numbers" (p. 35). Although investment "freely directed" might not be subject to diminishing returns, certainly, under static circumstances, continued investment in any one particular direction ought eventually to result in a declining rate of return. Yet, as T. W. Schultz (1973*b*) has emphasized, the rate of return appears to have diminished little, if at all, in response to a high level and even accelerated pace of investment in human capital, and, indeed, it may have actually risen (T. W. Schultz, 1971, p. 173).

We do not, of course, have any really accurate measure of the extent of investment in human capital as compared with investment in non-human capital and in the stock of knowledge through investment in research and development. Yet, there are a number of clues which suggest that the capital stock invested in human beings, even on a per capita basis, has been a steadily growing portion of the capital stock. T. W. Schultz (1961, p. 73) suggests a rise of the value of the stock of educational human capital embodied in the stock of labor of persons age fourteen and older from 18 percent in 1900 of the total educational and physical capital to 30 percent in 1957. These estimates do not include on-the-job training or investments in better health and nutrition. In terms of gross capital formation, Kuznets (1966, p. 243) calculates, on the basis of Schultz's earlier work, a rise in the share of investments in formal education alone from "about 9% in 1900 to over 38% in the 1950s." Moreover, for Western countries as a whole, Kuznets (1971) calculates the share of labor has risen from 55 to 75 percent of national income over the same period. These facts, meager as they may be, suggest two significant questions which are germane to the issue with which this paper began, namely, how can the new home economics be integrated into a general theory of economic growth and development in a manner which has some hope, at least, of bearing on the grand question of the demographic transition? These two questions are the following.

First, what accounts for the failure of the rate of return on investments in human capital, even counting educational investments, to fall, despite a high and accelerating rate of investment in this form of capital relative to other forms? In other words, why does there appear to be a persistent disequilibrium among these rates of return?

Second, quite apart from the possibility of disequilibrium rates of return (even if they are in equilibrium), what effect will increasing human capital investment per capita have on the allocation of resources within the household and what, if any, repercussions will it have for the rate of growth of population and labor force? A number of speculations and conjectures on the answers to these questions follow; they emphasize the role of the increasing value of human time over time and its relation, which is reciprocal, to the increasing level of investment in human beings.

Razin (1969, 1972) showed how, under certain circumstances, the ratio of human to total capital per capita would increase along the optimal growth path of an economy experiencing technical progress. As indicated earlier, T. W. Schultz has emphasized this aspect of the persistent failure of rates of return to investments in human capital to decline. The demand for skills and knowledge embodied in human capital does not decline because of additional investments in the stock of useful knowledge and technique (technological change) which require the continual adaptation and adjustment of the human agent to utilize efficiently this augmented stock and seek out the new sources of investment opportunities which maintain the growth process. But even in the absence of a persistent disequilibrium created by the demand for human capital, it is possible that the rates of return of such investments would fail to fall over time, or fall only slowly, in relation to the rates of return to other forms of investment because of endogenously changing relative cost of investment, that is, changes on the supply side.

One of the most important consequences of the growing "quality" of human beings as reflected in the increased stock of human capital per capita, as pointed out by T. W. Schultz (1973b), is the increasing value of human time per unit of such time. Many of the consequences of the increasing value of time over time are amusingly explored by Linder (1970) in his penetrating study of *The Harried Leisure Class.* Yet Linder and Schultz fail to note the important link which may exist between the increasing value of human time, due presumably to investment in human capital as well as to investment in other forms of capital and in technological change, and the terms on which investment in human capital takes place. If one assumes, as I think plausible, that children (as regards both quality and quantitiy) are time intensive as compared with other goods produced within the home, it follows that unless the increasing investment of human capital increases the marginal productivity of a unit of time in the care and rearing of children within the home in an offsetting fashion, increases in the value of time will lead to a shift away from children to less time-intensive activities. To be sure, such a substitution effect may be offset by a strong income effect, but here are still further grounds to suppose that both substitution and income effects will tend to lead to an increase in child quality rather than child number.

The investments in child quality referred to earlier take two major forms: (1) sound nutrition and health care, and (2) education, skills, or attitudes conducive to acquisition of further education and skills.

Good nutrition and health care increase youngsters' chances of survival and may also affect their ability to absorb future investments in intellectual capital. To the extent that such investments increase the life span, particularly the span of years over which a person can be economically active, such an increase in quality will raise the return to investments in human capital which sons and daughters may later wish to make in themselves. To the extent that better health and nutrition result in a reduction in child mortality, they increase the satisfactions accruing to parents from other forms of investment which also raise child quality, for the returns to these investments may then be expected to be enjoyed over a longer period of time on average. Increases in longevity, particularly of an individual's economically productive years, increase the amount of human time available without increasing population; such an increase would tend by itself to lower the value of time per unit, but, as we know, most of the effects of better health care and nutrition occur in childhood and enhance the quality of a unit of time in later years more than increasing the number of children. On net balance, therefore, I would conjecture that better health and nutrition lower the costs of further investments in human capital relative to those in other forms of capital and increase the returns therefrom.

The second main form which an increase in child quality may take is, as I have stated, through an investment in the form of education, skills, or attitudes conducive to later acquisition of further education or skills. Much investment in human capital of this type tends to be time intensive in the preschool years, although the productivity of a unit of a mother's time, as remarked, may be especially enhanced by a greater stock of human capital embodied in her, so it is not necessarily true that over time, as the result of the increasing value of human time, substitution will tend to occur away from this form of investment. Nonetheless, it is in this area that we might expect some induced "technological innovations" which could economize on a mother's scarce time. Nursery schools, day-care centers, and the proliferation of "educational" toys are perhaps examples. On the whole, then, I think we may conclude that increase in quality of children relative to their numbers take the form of investments in human capital which ultimately have the effect of raising the value of time per unit in the economically active years of adulthood.

The outlines of a revised Malthusian model begin to emerge, albeit dimly, from the foregoing conjectures and speculations. In this model, the value of human time and changes in that value over time are pivotal, and the limitations imposed by natural resources are mitigated, if not eliminated, by technological progress and increases in the stock of knowledge and of capital, both human and nonhuman. The main link between household and economy is the value of human time; the increased value of human time results in fewer children per household, with each child embodying greater investments in human capital which in turn result in lower mortality and greater productivity in the economically active years. Such greater productivity in turn further raises both the value of a unit of time and income in the subsequent generation and enables persons of that generation to make efficient use of new knowledge and new physical capital. Eventually, rates of return to investments in physical capital, new knowledge, and human capital may begin to equalize, but as long as investment occurs which increases the amount of human capital per individual, the value of a unit of human time must continue to increase. It is not possible to say whether the diminishing ability of a human being to absorb such investment would eventually stabilize the number of children per household and at what level, given the satisfactions parents obtain from numbers of children as well as their quality. Nonetheless, over time the model does predict in rough qualitative fashion declining rates of population growth (perhaps eventually zero rates or even negative rates for a time) and declining rates of infant mortality. These are the main features of the demographic transition.

NOTES

1. Jacob Mincer objected to this and said that the model should really be called the "Morningside Heights" model; however, force of habit leads me to persist in this terminology.
2. Unfortunately, to date relatively little attention has been paid to the implications of the household-production model for the more general

composition of consumption. Time and market-purchasable-commodity intensities do differ greatly for different types of consumption (e.g., drinking beer or going to a concert), and the new home economics has implications going beyond fertility and human capital formation (see, however, Michael [1972]).

3. Indeed, there is good reason to suppose that the reason for many institutions of society is precisely to ensure that the interests of future generations will be adequately guarded by the present. A meaningful theory of intergenerational welfare comparisons has not yet been developed, but such a theory is surely central to our understanding of household decision-making and its consequences.

4. Still, it may be helpful analytically to tackle the problem in a stepwise fashion (see Becker, 1973). In part of his work, Becker does consider the division of the gains from marriage, the most important gains being children, and this is, of course, a matter closely related to the utility function maximized within the marriage.

5. A partial exception is the work of Michael Grossman (1971; 1972, pp. 74-79). In his analysis Grossman does assume separate production processes but stipulates that the entire amounts of certain factors available to the household must enter each production function as one of its arguments. That is to say, in the standard analysis, if one could separately identify the amount of one factor—say, wife's time—used in a particular activity, one could measure the effect of a unit increase in that input on the output of that activity independently of the overall resource constraint on the wife's time to the household, whereas in Grossman's formulation the overhead factor, say, the family house, cannot in principle be allocated among the activities but must enter fully into each one. Grossman's work however, still does lack generality in the respect discussed above, since complementarity among final goods cannot be encompassed in his formulation except through the rather Ptolemaic device of introducing some of the final outputs as inputs in the production processes of some of the other outputs.

6. Much recent work, however, is dynamic only in the relatively trivial sense of involving maximization over a number of periods of time without uncertainty concerning the values of future values of exogenous constraints to future decisions. This is the sense in which a dynamic programming problem can be turned into an ordinary programming problem of much larger dimensions; apart from the computational difficulties thus introduced, the chief defect of this approach is that it fails to lay bare the sequential nature of the decision-making process in the way, for

example, in which the recursive solution to the general dynamic programming problem of Bellman does. In the absence of uncertainty, however, nothing essential is lost by the straightforward multiperiod extension of the basically static framework. When values of future constraints are uncertain, then it does become essential to understand and incorporate the sequential character of the decision process (see Nerlove, 1972*a*). So far this has not been done in the literature of the new home economics.

7. Closely connected to the matter of what is inherited from the past and transferred from generation to generation is the problem of how individual tastes and preferences are formed and how they may change over time. I have not mentioned this issue lest I be excommunicated from the economics profession! It is virtually part of the definition of what an economist is that he takes tastes as given, and I sometimes suspect that many of us require all tastes to be identical and assume that all differences among individuals arise from differences in the resource constraints those individuals face. Indeed, one of the consequences of the conjectures and speculations presented in Section 3 is that the tastes and preferences of at least different generations, if not of individuals within each generation, could remain constant while the number of children per family declined over time due to changes in the value of human time induced endogenously.

REFERENCES

Baumol, William J. *Economic Dynamics: An Introduction.* 3d ed. New York: Macmillan, 1970.

Becker, Gary S. "A Theory of the Allocation of Time." *Econ. J.* 75 (September 1965), 493-517.

———. "A Theory of Marriage: Part I." *J.P.E.* 81 (July/August 1973), 813-46.

Becker, Gary S., and Barry R. Chiswick. "Education and the Distribution of Earnings." *A.E.R.* 56 (May 1966), 358-69.

Ben-Porath, Yoram. "The Production of Human Capital and the Life Cycle of Earnings." *J.P.E.* 75 (August 1967), 352-65.

———. "Economic Analysis of Fertility in Israel: Point and Counterpoint." *J.P.E.* 81, no. 2, suppl. (March/April 1973), S202-233.

Cain, Glen G. *Married Women in the Labor Force: An Economic Analysis.* Chicago: Univ. Chicago Press, 1966.

DeTray, Dennis N. "Child Quality and the Demand for Children." *J.P.E.* 81, no. 2, suppl. (March/April 1973), S70-95.

Ghez, Gilbert R., and Gary S. Becker. "The Allocation of Time and Goods over the Life Cycle." Report no. 7,217. Chicago: Center Math. Studies Bus. and Econ., Univ. Chicago, April 1972.

Gorman, W. M. "Separability and Aggregation." *Econometrica* 27 (July 1959), 469-481.

Gronau, Reuben. "The Effect of Children on the Housewife's Value of Time." *J.P.E.* 81, no. 2, suppl. (March/April 1973), S168-99.

Grossman, Michael. "The Economics of Joint Production in the Household." Report no. 7,145. Chicago: Center Math. Studies Bus. and Econ., Univ. Chicago, September 1971.

Hall, Robert E. "Comment." *J.P.E.* 81, no. 2, suppl. (March/April 1973), S200-201.

Heckman, James J. "Three Essays on the Supply of Labor and the Demand for Market Goods." Ph.D. dissertation, Princeton Univ., 1971.

Knight, Frank H. *Risk, Uncertainty and Profit.* Boston: Houghton-Mifflin, 1921.

———. "Diminishing Returns from Investment." *J.P.E.* 52 (March 1944), 26-47.

———. *The Economic Organization.* New York: Harper & Row, 1965. (Originally published by the College of the University of Chicago, 1933.)

Koopmans, Tjalling C. "Intertemporal Distribution and 'Optimal' Aggregate Economic Growth." In W. Fellner et al., *Ten Economic Studies in the Tradition of Irving Fisher.* New York: Wiley, 1967.

Kuznets, Simon. *Modern Economic Growth: Rate, Structure, and Spread.* New Haven, Conn.: Yale Univ. Press, 1966.

———. *Economic Growth and Nations.* Cambridge, Mass.: Harvard Univ. Press, 1971.

Lancaster, Kelvin J. "A New Approach to Consumer Theory," *J.P.E.* 74 (April 1966), 132-157.

Leibowitz, Arleen. "Women's Allocation of Time to Market and Nonmarket Activities: Differences by Education." Ph.D. dissertation, Columbia Univ., 1972.

Leontief, W. "Introduction to a Theory of the Internal Structure of Functional Relationships." *Econometrica* 15 (October 1947), 361-373.

Linder, Staffan B. *The Harried Leisure Class.* New York: Columbia Univ. Press, 1970.

Malthus, T. R. *An Essay on the Principle of Population and a Summary View of the*

Principle of Population. Baltimore: Penguin, 1970. (Originally published in 1798 and 1830.)

Michael, Robert T. *The Effect of Education on Efficiency in Consumption.* Occasional Paper no. 116. New York: Nat. Bur. Econ. Res., 1972.

Michael, Robert T., and Gary S. Becker. "On the New Theory of Consumer Behavior." Mimeographed. New York: Nat. Bur. Econ. Res., December, 1972.

Mincer, Jacob. "Market Prices, Opportunity Costs, and Income Effects." In *Measurement in Economics: Studies in Mathematical Economics and Econometrics in Memory of Yehuda Grunfeld,* edited by Carl Christ et al. Stanford, Calif.: Stanford Univ. Press, 1963.

———. "The Distribution of Labor Incomes: A Survey with Special Reference to the Human Capital Approach." *J. Econ. Literature* 8 (March 1970), 1-26.

———. *Schooling, Experience, and Earnings.* New York: Nat. Bur. Econ. Res., 1974.

Mitchell, Wesley C. "The Backward Art of Spending Money." *A.E.R.* 2 (June 1912), 269-281.

Morishima, Michio. *Theory of Economic Growth.* 2d rev. impression. Oxford: Clarendon, 1970.

Muth, Richard F. "Household Production and Consumer Demand Functions." *Econometrica* 34 (July 1966), 699-708.

Nerlove, Marc. "Tuition and the Costs of Higher Education: Prolegomena to a Conceptual Framework." *J.P.E.* 80, no. 3, suppl. (May/June 1972), S178-218. (*b*)

Nerlove, Marc, and T. Paul Schultz. *Love and Life between the Censuses: A Model of Family Decision Making in Puerto Rico, 1950-1960.* RM-6322-AID. Santa Monica, Calif.: RAND Corp., September 1970.

O'Hara, Donald J. *Changes in Mortality Levels and Family Decisions regarding Children.* R-914-RF. Santa Monica, Calif.: RAND Corp., February 1972.

Pitchford, J. D. *Population in Economic Growth.* Mimeographed monograph. Canberra: Australian Nat. Univ., 1973.

Razin, Assaf. "Investment in Human Capital and Economic Growth: A Theoretical Study," Ph.D. dissertation, Univ. Chicago, 1969.

———. "Investment in Human Capital and Economic Growth." *Metoreconomica* 24 (May/August 1972), 101-116.

Reid, Margaret G. *Economics of Household Production.* New York: Wiley, 1934.

Samuelson, Paul A. "Social Indifference Curves." *Q.J.E.* 70 (February 1956), 1-22.

Schultz, Theodore W. "Education and Economic Growth." In *Social Forces Influencing American Education, 1961,* edited by Nelson B. Henry. Sixtieth yearbook of the National Society for the Study of Education, pt. 2. Chicago: Univ. Chicago Press, 1961.

———. *Investment in Human Capital.* New York: Free Press, 1971.

———. "The Increasing Economic Value of Human Time." *American J. Agricultural Econ.* 54 (December 1972), 843-50. (*b*)

———. "The Value of Children: An Economic Perspective." *J.P.E.* 81, pt. 2, suppl. (March/April 1973), S2-13. (*b*)

Smith, James P. "The Life Cycle Allocation of Time in a Family Context." Ph.D. dissertation, Univ. Chicago, 1972.

Solow, Robert M. "A Contribution to the Theory of Economic Growth." *Q.J.E.* 70 (February 1956), 65-94.

Strotz, R. "The Empirical Implications of a Utility Tree." *Econometrica* 25 (April 1957): 269-280.

———. "The Utility Tree—Correction and Further Appraisal." *Econometrica* 27 (July 1959), 482-488.

Swan, T. W. "Economic Growth and Capital Accumulation." *Econ. Record* 32 (November 1956), 334-361.

Sweet, James A. "Family Composition and the Labor Force Activity of Married Women in the United States." Ph.D. dissertation, Univ. Michigan, 1968.

Willis, Robert J. "A New Approach to the Economic Theory of Fertility Behavior." *J.P.E.* 81, pt. 2, suppl. (March/April 1973), S14-64.

PART II

Corporate Control
and Power

An important aspect of the evaluation of the corporation is the nature of the power possessed and exercised by it. Professor Galbraith has sketched a broad panorama in which he holds that large-size enterprise in a wide number of spheres results from technological scale economies and from the economies of planning. This large size, he states, has enabled large business corporations to plan and organize their activities free of the influence of the marketplace. He argues that they control the marketplace rather than using the marketplace as a source of signals for making production and output decisions. In the administration and operation of these large enterprises, operating in markets controlled for them by the government, Galbraith describes the behavior of business executives as essentially that of bureaucrats in any large-scale organization. Yet, at the same time, Galbraith urges that large corporate enterprise exercises great power. He holds that because of the importance of the government functions performed for business enterprise, corporate enterprise threatens to control government in its own self-interest.

As a solution to the problems raised in his latest book, *Economics and the Public Purpose,* Galbraith recommends socialization of a number of industries in the U.S. economy. Such a prescription demonstrates that the questions raised are indeed of very great economic, political, and social importance. The issue now posed by one of the influential writers of our time involves the very fundamentals of the organization of our society in terms not only of economic dimensions, but also in terms affecting the fundamental social and political fabric of the nation.

While the essays in Part II are not directed specifically toward an evaluation and assessment of the Galbraithian theories, they provide much important evidence relevant for assessing the important issues raised. The first essay, by Professor Williamson, is stimulated by the development of the internal organization and control processes in business firms. Indeed, an important aspect of the significance of the internal organization and control processes of business firms is that they represent efforts to adjust more rapidly and efficiently to changes in the economic and business environment. The effect of the development of internal organizational and control systems is to make the large corporate organization more responsive in adjusting to the market rather than less so, as Galbraith avers. Indeed, the development of internal organizational and control processes has been so important and so considerable as to require the modification, enrichment, and further development of conventional economic theory. The implication for economic theory of the development of the internal organization and control processes is the central theme of the essay by Professor Williamson. The remaining two papers deal with the questions of power raised by Galbraith and others.

Professor Williamson begins by summarizing the basic emphasis of received microeconomic theory. He observes that basic economic theory assumes that firms adopt the best way to produce goods and that they are guided by the goal of profit maximization. Economics describes the influence of different demand and supply conditions on output and prices. Conventional economics has ignored the broader, long-term aspects of planning strategies by business firms. In addition, it has failed to give adequate consideration to issues of corporate organization and internal control processes. The textbook models of the economy assume that a large number of firms is the natural condition for each industry, that there is no uncertainty in environment, and that there is perfect movement of factors and products on the basis of complete knowledge of market conditions. But even the conventional standard textbook approach to economics is beginning to recognize that the modern business firm is represented by the large corporation. However, it is held that competition between large corporations is limited by the dominance of one of a few corporations or collusion between them. Professor Williamson observes that this is an oversimplified picture of the world, and, particularly, of the behavior of the large corporation. He proposes a new approach to the analysis of business firm behavior by what he terms the "transactional" approach. The "transactional" approach emphasizes the internal organization and control processes of the large organization and analyzes what determines whether transactions take place across markets or within firms. He analyzes the conditions which result in market failure defined in the sense of circumstances under which markets are less efficient in performing transactions than transactions within individual firms. Professor Williamson emphasizes that real-world transactions take place under considerable uncertainty with regard to what is taking place both in the market as well as in group processes within the organization. He observes that rivalry takes place between a relatively small number of large organizations. In addition, there may be information disparities between buyers and sellers as well as between rivals.

Professor Williamson considers in some detail the problems of effectively managing a large-scale organization. He observes that there are limits to the extent to which individual managers can make calculations of what is going on in the market as well as keeping track of everything going on within the firm. He emphasizes that, in controlling the organization and internal processes of the large corporation, those with responsibility and control must recognize that they are dealing with individuals who will be motivated to a considerable degree by opportunism. Professor Williamson defines opportunism as self-interest with guile. He observes that this human characteristic is one of the influences which leads to the robustness of internal organization. Transactions within the firm may take place precisely because the internal organization of the firm may provide control instruments that may curb opportunistic proclivities at lower costs than achieved by markets. This is one rationale for transactions taking place within firms rather than across markets. Professor Williamson gives a number of illustrations of this principle and then goes on to describe how the transactional approach can explain certain phenomena in the economic world for which conventional economic theory is unable to provide a rationale. He takes up, in particular, the concepts of vertical integration and conglomerate organization.

With regard to vertical integration, one view holds that when vertical integration occurs, economic efficiency is the reason, and vertical integration as such cannot create monopoly power. In fact, it can provide the basis for important efficiency gains. One economic manifestation of this view is the industry life-cycle pattern of the use of vertical integration. In a new industry, there tends to be vertical integration because the volume is too small for specialized firms. As volume grows, some specialist functions performed by individual firms for the entire industry or for a number of industries can achieve a volume that will produce efficiencies and economies of scale that could not be attained if individual firms performed these functions themselves. As the rate of growth in the industry slows, reintegration may take place for the purpose of reducing costs as competition with other products, and an increasing number of substitutes appear.

In explaining how costs are reduced by integrated operations, standard microtheory was not well articulated. The transactional cost approach developed by Professor Williamson explains how costs can be reduced by vertical integration. There are three factors involved. One is that information may be exchanged more efficiently. Two is that in the exchange of physical components the necessity of negotiating contracts between a small number of bargainers is avoided. Third, growth leads to advantages of learning by experience which leads to organizations of increased efficiency. However, Professor Williamson observes that a barrier to entry in some sense is thereby created in that the necessity for having developed some capability over a range of activities causes greater risks for a potential new entrant.

The transactional approach also enables Professor Williamson to analyze the conglomerate firm phenomenon. His rationale for conglomerate firms is that the conglomerate serves both to supply performance-related incentives to corporate managers and to reallocate resources from what in an economy of specialized firms would frequently be put to lower than higher-yield purposes. Professor Williamson considers the theory that large conglomerates confronting one another in several markets may practice mutual forbearance and be less competitive than smaller or regional firms. The evidence for this claim, he states, is rather limited and much of it is inapposite. Professor Williamson concludes that over the long pull, competition will sort out the conglomerates which possess coherent internal structures from those which do not.

But increasing emphasis in appraising the conglomerate firm has been less on economic considerations than on the potential political power that they may exercise. The issue of power in America and the role of the large corporation is developed in the next paper by Professor Richard Posner. Professor Posner begins with an analysis of the implications of the perfect competition model. He points out that the perfect competition model omits many important aspects of the real world and has deficiencies for analyzing the broader issues relating to power. The perfect competiton model emphasizes that an industry, a considerable portion of whose output is accounted for by a small number of firms, has been characterized by the term *oligopoly*. The perfect competition model generally can be used to argue that the existence of a small number of firms facilitates and may lead to tacit collusion. Professor Posner observes that the evidence on this issue is moot. He then observes even if tacit collusion did occur, there are no implications of such behavior for a debate over corporate power. Further, he observes that the people who attack big business on monopoly grounds do not criticize unions or the minimum wage. It appears that their objections are to big business and not to monopolization as such.

Professor Posner next considers whether advertising enables business to exercise power over the consumer. He reasons that since business firms spend money on them, the advertising messages must have some effect. Thus, the taste of the public must be affected. Professor Posner observes that even though firms in advertising may be seeking to change consumers' tastes, it does not follow that advertising in the aggregate will, in fact, change consumers' tastes. Since advertisers are competing with one another for the consumer's dollars, to a considerable extent the many efforts to change consumer's tastes are neutralizing. To some degree, the motive for advertising by business firms is a defensive measure. Advertising has also been criticized as a waste.

Professor Posner observes that here as well as in a number of other areas, the corporation is accused of all of the vices that are said to result from efforts to maximize profits while at the same time they are accused of vices, such as slackness or yielding to unreasonable union demands, that result from failure to pursue the goal of profit maximization.

The most serious criticism against the large corporation is the allegation that it uses the political process to further its private ends. But the criticism applies more broadly. In a political democracy particular interest groups have developed to attempt to shape public policy. Professor Posner argues that the role of interest groups in shaping public policy does not provide a basis for criticisms of large corporations as such. He notes that the subordination of consumer to producer interests in the production of legislation seems independent of the size of individual firms involved. We observe as much or more protective legislation in small-business industries such as agriculture, textiles, and trucking as in large-firm industries.

Professor Posner notes, particularly in an analysis of the impact of conglomerate corporations, that bigness itself is not sufficient to assure protective legislation. He observes that they were unable to prevent adverse legislation from being enacted with regard to their antitrust treatment and accounting practices. Because conglomerates by nature are highly diversified, they do not have common economic interests and have interests that conflict with many other firms with which they compete. Thus within each conglomerate firm there are divergent interests that limit its ability to take a unitary position on a particular legislation. For example, high tariffs might help one branch of the enterprise, but hurt others that utilize imported inputs. Posner advances the theory that the number of workers in an industry may be a more reliable forecaster of the magnitude of its political power than the number of firms in the industry.

Finally, Professor Posner considers the reasons for the widely held negative attitude toward big business. He ascribes it to a number of influences. (1) A lack of understanding of the operation of the market system. (2) A vested interest in disparaging the operation of the market system because of the preference for central planning. (Note in this connection Galbraith's recommendation for socialization of a number of sectors of the economy.) (3) A sociological need to have a sinister force to be used as an explanation for economic and political ills. It is in this connection that the emerging multinational corporations have an increasing role to play. They are therefore next considered in the analysis.

In the paper by Professors Robbins and Stobaugh, the emerging tensions between the multinational corporations and individual host countries are examined. The nature and management aspects of the multinational corporation are first considered. The ability of the large multinational enterprise to transfer resources within its different operations is the key to the success of the multinational corporation. At the same time, it is the focus of conflict between the corporation and the state. The multinational enterprise is a system that performs best when its management is aware of the opportunities growing out of the financial ties that link the system together. To take advantage of these opportunities, management commands a common pool of resources that can be moved through the system's binding links from one unit to another in accordance with a well-designed strategy.

Professors Robbins and Stobaugh indicate the requirements for successful operations by multinational corporations. They observe that management must utilize the systems approach in planning corporate objectives on a global basis. They must utilize the multinational firm's unique advantages over domestic companies in adjusting to currency relationships, differences in interests costs, and differences in tax rates throughout the world. They observe that from their studies only about a third of the multinational enterprises analyzed pursue such a systems strategy designed to optimize the corporation's profit potential. Thus, the typical multinational firm has considerable room for improvement in operations and is moving in this direction. The pace is slow because of inherent difficulties in achieving adjustment in far-flung installations as well as the jarring effects of resolving presumed differences between the interests of the corporations and of the local governments.

Large multinational corporations hold a large amount of assets. In 1971, for example, U.S. multinationals held some $25 billion in cash items plus $100 billion in inventory and accounts receivable. Because of these large asset holdings, multinational corporations are often seen as a threat to a country's financial stability. However, Professors Robbins and Stobaugh observe that the multinational corporations do not move their funds in unison. Of course, within the multinational system, it is common for headquarters to order a subsidiary located in a country with shaky currency to immediately pay off its intercompany account, but to order the other affiliates to defer their payments to that subsidiary. From the defensive state of seeking to avoid a translation or conversion loss, it is difficult to distinguish from practices that represent movement into the speculative arena where the emphasis is on seeking currency profits. It may not be easy to discern whether a buildup of current assets in a strong-currency country is done for protective or speculative reasons.

Despite fears about the financial impact of the operation of the multinational companies, Professors Robbins and Stobaugh see them performing an increasingly important role. They hold that worldwide industrial progress is dependent on the scientific and business technologies disseminated by multinational enterprise. There is simply no other economic entity in sight to take on this job in the world where markets are international and the key for entrance into these markets is technology. They depict a scenario which calls for continued growth of corporate multinational firms that increasingly desire freedom to shuttle resources within the orbits of their own systems. Opposed to them are the nation-states ready to impose restrictions on these movements whenever they sense a threat to their financial position.

One alternative would be the creation of international arbitrator. However, such an overseer for the affairs of multinational corporations would not be appealing to either the enterprise or the state. Multinational enterprises would not be eager to have another regulatory body with which to contend. Nations would be reluctant to surrender their right to control businesses within their boundaries. Thus, Robbins and Stobaugh predict that there will be increased bargaining between the corporate multinational firms and the political states.

The multinational enterprise will increasingly seek permission to shift resources and will use as its bargaining lever the capital and technology that it could introduce into the country. The state will agree to a designated degree of mobility, dependent upon its need for fresh supplies of capital and technology as well as upon its own economic position. Thus, a critical executive skill for the multinational corporation will be the ability to negotiate with countries to obtain the necessary freedom to carry out and to realize the potentials of the multinational corporation.

Thus, Part II of this book provides an overview of the internal organization and operations of the individual firm both domestic and multinational in orientation. Some of the power implications of large firms are then analyzed. Finally, the large firm is critically examined in its international dimensions.

THREE

Assessing the Modern Corporation: Transaction Cost Considerations

Oliver E. Williamson

Professor of Economics
University of Pennsylvania

Academic: S.B., Massachusetts Institute of Technology, 1955; M.B.A., Stanford, 1960; Ph.D., Carnegie Institute of Technology, 1963. Doctoral Dissertation: "The Economics of Discretionary Behavior: Managerial Objectives in a Theory of the Firm," 1963.

Publications: *The Economics of Discretionary Behavior: Managerial Objectives in a Theory of the Firm,* 1964; "Hierarchical Control and Optimum Firm Size," *Journal of Political Economy,* 1967; "Wage Rates as a Barrier to Entry: The Pennington Case in Perspective," *Quarterly Journal of Economics,* 1968.

Research: Corporate Control and Business Behavior; Aspects of Monopoly Theory and Policy; assistant professor, economics, University of California, Berkeley, 1963-65; special economic assistant to assistant attorney general, Antitrust U.S. Department of Justice, 1966-67; associate professor of economics, University of Pennsylvania, 1965-68, professor of economics since 1968.

I will attempt in this chapter to contrast what I refer to as the transaction cost approach to the theory of the firm with received microtheory on the one hand and populist critiques of the modern corporation on the other. While the transaction cost approach that I favor represents, I think, a relatively "new" way of examining a variety of long-standing problems,[1] it is scarcely unfamiliar to many economists who, in their own work, have been expressly concerned with transactional considerations for a number of years. I begin with a brief statement of the transaction cost approach to the study of business behavior. Vertical integration and conglomerate organization issues are then examined in Sections 2 and 3, respectively. Concluding remarks follow.

1. THE TRANSACTION COST APPROACH

The transactional approach may be characterized succinctly as follows: (1) markets and firms are alternative instruments for completing a related set of transactions; (2) whether a set of transactions ought to be executed across markets or within a firm depends on the efficiency properties of each mode; (3) the costs of writing and executing complex contracts across a market turns on the characteristics of the human decision-makers who are involved with the transaction on the one hand, and the objective properties of the market on the other; (4) although the human and transactional factors which impede exchanges across a market manifest themselves somewhat differently within the firm, the same set of factors apply to both. A symmetrical analysis of trading thus requires that the transactional limits of internal organization as well as the sources of market failure be acknowledged. Relevant in this regard is the following proposition: just as market structure matters in assessing the efficacy of trades in the marketplace, so likewise does internal structure matter when assessing internal organization.

The transaction cost approach is interdisciplinary in that it draws extensively on contributions from both economics and organization theory. The market failure,[2] contingent claims contracting,[3] and recent organizational design [4] literatures supply the requisite economic background. The administrative man [5] and strategic behavior [6] literatures are the main organization theory inputs.

It is commonly convenient, and is here, to identify a reference condition under which exchange is assumed initially to take place. Though hardly historically accurate, the reference condition which I favor, which is consistent with the biases of economists, is to assume that "in the beginning there were markets." The transaction cost approach attempts to identify a set of market or *transactional factors* which together with a related set of *human factors* explain the circumstances under which complex contingent claims contracts will be difficult to write, execute, and enforce. Markets in these circumstances will be prone to distortion,[7] in which case hierarchical modes of organization warrant consideration.

The transactional factors which lead to prospective market failure are uncertainty, small numbers exchange relations, and information disparities (which I will sometimes refer to as a condition of "information impactedness") among the parties.[8] Unless joined, however, by a related set of human factors, such transactional conditions need not impede market exchange. The human factors to which I would call particular attention, for the purposes of this paper, are bounded rationality and the proclivity of human actors to behave opportunistically. The implications of bounded rationality and opportunism for the organization of economic activity are both pervasive and important. However impressive in other respects it may be, a study of firms and markets which neglects these factors is, I submit, incomplete and possibly superficial.

Herbert Simon defines the principle of bounded rationality as follows: *"The capacity of the human mind for formulating and solving complex problems is very small compared with the size of the problems whose solution is required for objectively rational behavior in the real world."* [9] Bounded rationality refers to neurophysiological limits on the one hand (which take the form of rate and storage limits on the powers of individuals to receive, store, retrieve, and process information without error), and language limits on the other. A leading reason why internal organization supplants the market is because it serves to economize on the bounded rationality attributes of decision-makers in circumstances where prices are not "sufficient statistics" and adaptive, sequential decision-making under uncertainty is involved.[10]

Opportunism is an effort to realize individual gains through a lack of candor or honesty in transactions. It is not related to the conventional assumption of self-interest seeking in economics, but it is more subtle than self-interest seeking as this is usually described. Opportunism is self-interest seeking *with guile.* Such inclinations have organizational significance when paired with small numbers and information disparity conditions in markets. Internal organization arises in such circumstances because it alters incentives and permits a wider set of control instruments to be brought systematically to bear, thereby curbing the opportunistic proclivities of human actors, than the market affords at comparable cost.[11]

Merely to establish that markets experience exchange difficulties, however, does not imply that the transactions in question ought to be executed internally instead. For one thing, as previously noted, internal organization must contend with the same types of human and transactional factors that beset markets. Of special relevance in this connection are the following two propositions: (1) the limitations of internal organization in both bounded rationality and opportunistic respects vary directly with firm size, organization form held constant, but (2) organization form—i.e., the way in which activities in the firm are hierarchically structured—matters.[12]

I would furthermore note that, once made, the choice between firm and market ought not to be regarded as fixed. Both firms and markets change over time in ways which may render an initial assignment inappropriate. The degree of uncertainty associated with the transactions in question may diminish; market growth may support large numbers of supply relations; and information disparities between the parties often shrink. Also, changes in technology may occur which alter the degree to which bounded rationality limits apply, with the result that a different assignment of activities between markets and hierarchies than was selected initially later becomes indicated. The efficacy of completing transactions by one mode rather than another thus ought to be reassessed periodically—although firms (and bureaucracies more generally) are notoriously reluctant to give up functions once these have been assumed.

As compared with received microtheory, the transaction cost approach to the theory of the firm is much more microanalytic in its emphasis. Moreover, efficient adaptation to changing market circumstances, rather than static or comparative static analyses of equilibrium relations, is the focus of analysis. These differences are hopefully made apparent in the discussions of vertical integration and conglomerate organization, which follow.[14]

2. VERTICAL INTEGRATION

Under conventional assumptions that the costs of operating competitive markets are zero, "as is usually assumed in our theoretical analysis," [15] vertical integration is an anomaly. It is nevertheless a conspicuous fact of industrial life, and has been the object of recurrent attention by economists of both received microtheory and populist persuasions. My attention here will be restricted to analyses of the received microtheory type; populist positons are much less fully articulated on this issue.

2.1 Received Microtheory, General

In setting out what I think to be the main distinctions between the conventional and transactional approaches, I concede at the outset that my discussion of received microtheory is somewhat of a caricature. It is the theory of the firm as this appears in the conventional intermediate price theory textbook. Inasmuch as I find such a tactic often to be a source of considerable irritation in reviewing the work of others who have been concerned with studying the behavior of the modern corporation, I resort to it with some reluctance. My defense of such a procedure is that it is an economical way by which to get the issues exposed.

Received microtheory treats the firm as a productive unit committed to profit maximization. The firm here is essentially reduced to a production function.[16] Technological considerations thereby become dominant. Notions of business strategy and tactics or of corporate structure and internal control processes, by contrast, have little place and rarely appear.

The resulting construction permits the analyst to examine such issues as increasing returns to scale, the effect of sales taxes or changing factor prices, spillover effects (both positive and negative), and the like. This is a considerable achievement. But it also involves a sacrifice. Among other things, as Peter Diamond has noted, standard "economic models . . . [treat] individuals as playing a game with fixed rules which they obey. They do not buy more than they know they can pay for, they do not embezzle funds, they do not rob banks." [17] Expressed in terms of the language introduced in the preceding section, managers of firms (and other economic actors) are not opportunistic. Standard models also, as Herbert Simon has repeatedly emphasized, impute considerable power of computation and analysis to economic actors [18]—which is to say that bounded rationality rarely is thought to pose a problem. The transaction cost approach relaxes both of these behavioral assumptions.

While there is no necessary connection, those who rely exclusively on the received microtheory model of the firm are prone to express considerable confidence in the efficacy of competition. Problems of small numbers supply and of adapting efficiently to uncertainty are apt to be dismissed or settled in a rather artificial fashion. The upshot is that many of the interesting problems of economic organization are either finessed or dealt with in a dogmatic way.

2.2 Stigler on Vertical Integration [19]

George Stigler's explication, as it applies to vertical integration, of Adam Smith's theorem that "the division of labor is limited by the extent of the market" leads him to deduce the following life-cycle implications: vertical integration will be extensive in firms in young industries; disintegration will be observed as an industry grows; and reintegration will occur as an industry passes into decline. These life-cycle effects are illustrated by reference to a multiprocess product, each process involving a separable technology and hence has its own distinct cost function. (Stigler employs the separability assumption for conven-ience; relaxing it complicates but does not alter the general argument.) Some of the processes display individually falling cost curves; others rise continually; and still others have U-shaped cost curves. Stigler then inquires: Why does not the firm exploit the decreasing cost activities by expanding them to become a monopoly?

He answers by observing that, at the outset, the decreasing cost functions are "too small to support a specialized firm or firms." [20] But, unless the argument is meant to be restricted to global or local monop-olies, for which there is no indication, resort to a specialized firm does not exhaust the possibilities. Assuming that there are at least several rival firms in the business, why does not one of these exploit the available economies, to the mutual benefit of all the parties by producing the entire requirement for the group? The reasons, I submit, turn on transaction cost consideration.

If, for example, the exchange of information between the parties is involved (Stigler specifically refers to "market information" as one of the decreasing cost possibilities) strategic misrepresentation issues are posed. The risk here is that the specialist firm will disclose information to its rivals in an incomplete and distorted manner. Since the party buying the information can establish its accuracy only at great cost, possibly by collecting the original data itself, the exchange fails to go through. Were it, however, that rivals were not given to being opportunistic, the risk of strategic distortion would vanish and the (technologically efficient) specialization of information could proceed.

The exchange of physical components that experience decreasing costs is likewise discouraged where both long-term and spot-market contracts prospectively incur transactional difficulties. Long-term con-tracts are principally impeded by bounded rationality considerations: given bounded rationality, the extent to which uncertain future events can be expressly taken into account—in the sense that appropriate adaptations thereto are costed out and contractually specified—is simply limited. Since, given opportunism, incomplete long-term contracts predictably pose interest conflicts between the parties, other arrangments are apt to be sought.

Spot-market contracting is an obvious alternative. Such contracts, however, are hazardous if a small numbers supply relation obtains—which, by assumption, holds for the circumstances described by Stigler. The buyer then incurs the risk that the purchased product or service will, at some stage, be supplied under monopolistic terms. Industry growth, moreover, need not eliminate the tension of small numbers bargaining if the item in question is one for which learning by doing is important and the market for human capital is imperfect.[21] Delaying own-production until own-requirements are sufficient to exhaust scale economies would, considering the learning costs of undertaking own-production at this later time, incur substantial transition costs. It may, under these conditions, be more attractive from the outset for each firm to produce its own requirement—or, alternatively, for mergers to occur. Absent present or prospective transaction costs of the sorts described, however, specialization by one of the firms (i.e., monopoly supply), to the mutual benefit of all, would presumably occur. Put differently, technology is no bar to contracting; it is transactional considerations that are decisive.

2.3 The Condition of Entry

Stigler observes that "it is possible that vertical integration increases the difficulty of entry by new firms, by increasing the capital and knowledge necessary to conduct several types of operation rather than depend on rivals for supplies or markets."[22] But why, one might ask, ought increasing capital requirements by reason of vertical integration, alter the *terms* under which capital becomes available? And unless the terms are worsened, wherein lies the impediment?

A simple answer would be to respond that borrowing by the firm to finance additional plant and equipment is analogous to borrowing by the consumer to mortgage a house. I submit, however, that the analogy is at best imperfect. The firm is borrowing funds in anticipation of realizing a prospective stream of earnings. These prospective earnings, as well as the resale value of the assets in question, are used to support the loan in question. The homeowner, by contrast, is not ordinarily able to augment his earnings by his purchase of a house. Thus, whereas the householder who successively increases the size of his mortgage eventually incurs adverse capital costs, because the risks of default are greater, the firm need not likewise be impeded. Wherein, then, if at all, does vertical integration by established firms disadvantage prospective entrants on account of capital market "defects"?

Robert Bork observes in this connection that "In general, if greater than competitive profits are to be made in an industry, entry should occur whether the entrant has to come in at both levels or not. I know of no theory of imperfections in the capital market which would lead suppliers of capital to avoid areas of higher return to seek areas of lower return." [23] Similarly, Ward Bowman contends that "difficulties of access to the capital market that enable X to offer a one dollar inducement (it has a bankroll) and prevent its rivals from responding (they have no bankroll, and, though offering of the inducement is a responsible business tactic, for some reason cannot borrow the money) . . . [have] yet to be demonstrated." [24] As I hope to make apparent, these and related arguments of the received microtheory variety go through only if transaction cost considerations are suppressed.

It will be useful, for purposes of examining such contentions, to set out a specific example. In particular, suppose that the leading color film producer has integrated forward into film processing. The issue to be evaluated then is whether, for reasons relating to the cost of capital, a potential entrant who has developed a technologically satisfactory substitute and has an established production-related reputation will be discouraged from entering because, to come in, new investment at both color film production and processing stages must be arranged. If Bork and Bowman are correct, the following conditions ought to be regarded by the capital market with indifference: (1) the monopolistic producer is not integrated, in which case the prospective new entrant can enter into the production stage alone and utilize the processing facilities (suitably expanded if necessary) of existing processors, versus (2) the monopolistic producer is integrated and (a) the new entrant comes in at both stages, or (b) independent new entrants appear simultaneously at both the production and processing stages.

To contend that the terms of finance are the same under 2(a) as they are under 1 implies that the capital market has equal confidence in the new entrant's qualifications to perform processing activities as it does in firms that are already experienced in the business. Except in circumstances where experienced firms are plainly inept, this is tantamount to saying that experience counts for nought. This, however, is implausible for transactions that involve large, discrete rather than small but recurring commitments of funds. Thus, although transactions of the latter type can be monitored on the basis of ex post experience reasonably effectively, this is much less easy for transactions of the large, discrete variety—which are the kind under consideration here. Reputation, which is to say prior experience, is of special importance in establishing the terms of finance for transactions that involve large, discrete commitments of funds.

The reasons for this are to be traced in part in the incompleteness of information regarding the qualifications of applicants for financing. Faced with incomplete information, suppliers of capital are vulnerable to opportunistic representations. Unable to distinguish between those unknown candidates who have the capacity and the will to execute the project successfully from opportunistic types who assert that they are similarly qualified, when objectively (omnisciently) they are not, the terms of finance are adjusted adversely against the entire group. Hence, as between two candidates for financing, both of whom would be judged by an omniscient assessor to have identical capacities and wills to execute the project, but only one of whom has a favorable and widely known performance record, the unknown candidate will find that he is disadvantaged.

Furthermore, where both candidates are equally suspect, but one has access to internal sources of financing while the other does not, the candidate requiring outside financing may be unable to proceed. Timing, in this connection, can be of special significance. If one firm moves to the integrated structure gradually and finances the undertaking out of internal funds, while the second firm perceives the market opportunity later but, to be viable, must move immediately to a comparably integrated structure, the second firm may have to contend with adverse capital market rates.

The problems, moreover, do not vanish if the new entrant comes in at the production stage only and relies on independent entry into processing to occur. (The comparison here is condition 2(b) in relation to condition 1.) Not only is the cost of capital adjusted adversely against would-be new processors here, by reason of the lack of experience referred to above, but simultaneous yet independent entry into both stages may be impeded because of "nonconvergent expectations" [25]—which is to say that there is a risk that interdependent decisions between stages will fail to be made in a compatible way. Lack of common information among producers and processors with respect to market opportunities, investment intentions, or interfirm performance qualifications are the apparent impediments to effective coordination. Ultimately, however, the problems are to be attributed to bounded rationality, opportunism, and information impactedness.

To be sure, the argument has no special monopoly power significance unless the industry in question is already very concentrated—which, provisionally, I take to be any industry for which the four-firm concentration ratio exceeds 80 percent—or, in less concentrated markets, conditions of effective collusion, which include collective refusal to deal, obtain. In such circumstances, however, actual competition, by itself, cannot be expected to self-police the market in a way that reliably assures the competitive outcome. Accordingly, potential competition has an important role to play. If potential entrants regard imitation of prevailing vertical structures as contributing importantly to the prospect of successful entry (as they may in highly concentrated industries), vertical restrictions that require funds to be raised from less rather than more experienced sources can have entry-impeding consequences.

The argument thus reduces to the following: the capital market will finance the successful experienced firm on better terms than it will the average inexperienced firm and, probably, on better terms than it will any inexperienced firm whatsoever. That it is perceived to be better than the average is because of (1) objective cost advantages (see below), and (2) the existence among would-be new entrants of opportunistic types who are lacking in qualifications but who cannot, on account of information impactedness, be distinguished ex ante from more highly qualified types. These poorly qualified but opportunistic types pull the average down.

Suppose, however, that attention were somehow to be restricted to the more well-qualified types. What advantage has the experienced firm over these? Patent and related considerations aside, the superiority of the experienced firms here is a result of learning by doing cost advantages together with the imperfect transferability of the human factors in question. If the knowledge gleaned from experience is factor specific, which is to say deeply impacted, while the factors which have benefited are incompletely mobile (due partly to the fact that the benefits accrue sometimes to a *team* of related individuals, negotiating the transfer of which is prohibitively costly), the new entrant is plainly at a disadvantage. Information impactedness and imperfect labor markets thus combine to explain the cost disadvantage of the otherwise qualified new entrant in relation to the experienced firm. Assuming that the cost of capital varies inversely with the prospective profitability of the incremental investment, the experienced firm enjoys the edge.

2.4 Price Discrimination

Suppose, arguendo, that vertical market restrictions have no entry inhibiting consequences. Does the mobilization of latent monopoly power through vertical market restrictions then yield allocative efficiency gains, as Bork and Bowman contend?

I submit that, while it can and often does, it need not. Consider in this connection the standard comparison between pricing monopoly output at a single uniform price to all customers and the practice of perfect price discrimination. The usual verdict is that perfect price discrimination yields an unambiguous allocative efficiency gain over the uniform price that a nondiscriminating but otherwise profit-maximizing monopolist would charge.[26] But this result is reached under some rather restrictive assumptions: the costs of both discovering true customer valuations for the product and of enforcing restrictions that all sales shall be final are disregarded. Such costs vanish, however, only if either (1) customers honestly self-reveal preferences and self-enforce nonresale promises (i.e., an absence of opportunism is assumed), or (2) the seller is omniscient (which assumes unbounded rationality and the absence of information asymmetries).

Inasmuch as the assumptions needed to support the zero transaction cost assumption are plainly unrealistic, the question naturally arises: Does the argument go through when nontrivial transaction costs must be incurred to discover true customer valuations and police nonresale restrictions? Unfortunately for received microtheory, it does not.

That perfect price discrimination in the face of transaction costs need not yield a welfare gain can be seen by observing that the additional revenues realized by shifting from a uniform price monopoly position to one of fully discriminating monopoly exceed the associated welfare gains.[27] Consequently, while the monopolist may be prepared to incur the customer information and policing costs necessary to support such a shift (the incremental revenues exceed the associated costs), this same expenditure may exceed the welfare gains. An allocative efficiency loss, but a private monopoly gain, is therefore consistent with perfect price discrimination in circumstances where nontrivial transaction costs are incurred in reaching the discriminatory result.

Accordingly, those who contend the perfect price discrimination unambiguously yields an allocative efficiency gain must temporize. Transaction cost considerations reveal such a position to be overdrawn. The argument, moreover, is not saved by resorting to incomplete price discrimination of the familiar "third degree" variety.[28] Discrimination of this kind need not yield welfare gains—even under the assumption that transaction costs are negligible. The purported welfare gains of such incomplete price discrimination are, perforce, all the more suspect if transaction costs of the types described are believed to be significant. Consequently, Bowman's *general* conclusion that partial price discrimination has beneficial welfare effects and hence "is not an appropriate target for proscription under either antitrust or patient law"[29] cannot be maintained. The welfare results can simply not be established by appealing to standard microtheory models which assume away what may be an important part of the problem.[30]

3. CONGLOMERATE ORGANIZATION

There is not, to my knowledge, a well-developed position on conglomerates based on received microtheory. If vertical integration is regarded as an anomaly, under conventional assumptions, the conglomerate is even more deviant. The prevailing opinion among those who rely most extensively on received microtheory appears to be that the conglomerate is innocent of anticompetitive purpose and potential and ought not to be an object of antitrust prosecution.[31]

The populist critics of the conglomerate, however, are both numerous and vociferous. Robert Solo's position is perhaps representative. He contends that "when faced with a truly dangerous phenomenon, such as the conglomerate mergers of the 1960's, produced by financial manipulators making grist for their security mills, the professional antitrust economists were silent. Like other realities of a modern enterprise, this phenomenon, which will probably subvert management effectiveness and organizational rationale for generations, is outside their conceptual framework." [32]

Several things should be said in this connection. First, in defense of antitrust economists, I would point out that financial manipulation is not their main concern. This is the principal business of the Securities and Exchange Commission rather than the Antitrust Division. Although Solo might object, with cause, that economists are excessively narrow, it is nevertheless the security specialists who, as matters are divided up currently, are presumably at fault. Second, and more important, Solo's sweeping charges leave the particular dangers of the conglomerate phenomenon completely unspecified. Third, I agree that an understanding of the conglomerate requires an extension of the conventional framework. I nevertheless think it noteworthy that populist critics of the conglomerate and received microtheorists are alike in that *both* regard the firm in essentially technological terms. Finally, conglomerates come in a variety of forms and have a variety of purposes. Accordingly, a selective rather than a broadside attack on conglomerates is indicated.

The initial response of rival firms and financial analysts to an organizational innovation is typically to disregard it. Partly this is because "reorganization" is a common reaction by firms that are experiencing adversity. Discerning whether the response is intended to eliminate accumulated bureaucratic deadwood, to buy time from the stockholders by giving the impression that corrective action has been taken, or, instead or in addition, represents a really fundamental change in structure that warrants more widespread attention is initially unclear.[33] Expressed in institutional-failure terms, the problem is that opportu-

nistic structural changes cannot easily be distinguished from fundamental ones on account of information incompleteness and bounded
rationality. Given the incapacity (or high cost) of communicating
about, and abstractly assessing the importance of, organizational
changes, the tendency is to wait and see how organizational changes
manifest themselves in performance consequences. Inasmuch as performance is a function of many factors other than organizational
structure alone, sorting this out is difficult. Accordingly, a long recognition lag between fundamental innovation and widespread imitation is
common.[34]

Public policy analysts of populist persuasions are prone to regard
organizational innovations as having anticompetitive purposes. Rarely
are such innovations thought to have possible efficiency consequences,
mainly because efficiency is thought to reside in technological rather
than transactional factors. Ronald Coase, in a related connection,
makes the following observation: preoccupied as they are with monopoly problems, if a public policy analyst finds something "that he does
not understand, he looks for a monopoly explanation. And as in this field
we are very ignorant, the number of ununderstandable practices tends
to be very large, and the reliance on a monopoly explanation,
frequent." [35]

I have attempted elsewhere to examine the underlying rationality for
the conglomerate structure.[36] Essentially, the argument reduces to the
proposition that conglomerate firms (of the appropriate kind) [37] function as miniature capital markets. The conglomerate serves both to
supply performance-related incentives to corporate managers and to
reallocate resources from what, in an economy of specialized firms,
would frequently be put to lower- rather than to higher-yield purposes.

This poses an interesting dilemma, however: in comparison with the
banking system, the number of alternatives actively considered by the
conglomerate is relatively limited. Under conventional assumptions
that more choices are always better than fewer, the banking system
ought presumably to be an even more preferred resource allocation
mechanism. Were it that decision-makers could be efficiently apprised
of an ever wider range of alternatives and choose intelligently among
them, this would plainly be the case. But it is elementary that, where
complex, multidimensional choices are involved, as presumably they

are in these circumstances, information-processing capacities are quickly reached. As a result, expanding the range of choice may not only be without purpose but can have net detrimental effects. A tradeoff between breadth of information, in which respect the banking system may be presumed to have the advantage, and depth of information, which is the advantage of the (medium-sized) specialized firm, is thus involved. The conglomerate can be regarded as a compromise solution that, ideally, optimizes with respect to the breadth-depth tradeoff.[38] Although the number of alternatives considered is limited, its knowledge (ex post and ex ante) with respect to each remains relatively deep.

While I concede that not all conglomerates have adopted the "appropriate" internal structure to accomplish effective resource allocation and operating efficiency purposes, I am inclined to rely on the proposition that, over the long pull, competition in the product and capital markets will sort out the conglomerates which possess coherent internal structures from those that do not. If indeed this were to obtain, and assuming that the rationality properties that Weston [39] and I have imputed to conglomerates actually obtain, conglomerates ought presumably to be regarded more sympathetically by the antitrust agencies. Consider the following hypothetical exchange:

> Prospective Conglomerate: "What would you say, Mr. Assistant Attorney General, if the corporation could be devised that realized technological economies within each of its parts, facilitated the transfer process by which new developments of small firms are brought successfully to completion, served to mobilize competition in the capital market, yet in no market has a substantial market share?"
>
> Mr. Assistant Attorney: "Great."

The usual populist attitude toward the conglomerate is nevertheless one of skepticism or thinly disguised hostility. Harlan Blake's recent review of the policy implications of the conglomerate is perhaps representative.[40] Like Solo, his treatment tends to be global rather than selective. Consider the following:

> (1) He makes no organization form distinctions. Size considerations aside, all conglomerates are treated as an undifferentiated

group. But there are indications that even the courts may be more discriminating than this. (Thus the Connecticut court in the *ITT-Hartford Insurance* case was prepared to dismiss reciprocity arguments by the government because of organized form considerations.) [41]

(2) While Blake recognizes that the conglomerate may have had invigorating effects on the market for corporate control,[42] he does not regard its ability to reallocate assets internally to high-yield uses as a favorable factor. If anything, he seems to suggest that internal resource allocations are undesirable.[43] In an economy, however, where returning funds to and reallocating funds by the capital market incurs nontrivial transaction costs and/or managers of specialized firms opportunistically display positive-earnings retention preferences, the internal allocation of resources to high-yield uses is what most commends the conglomerate as compared with similarly constituted specialized firms. The conglomerate in these circumstances assumes miniature capital market responsibilities of an energizing kind. That Blake is unimpressed with such consequences is explained by his assessment (which he shares with conventional microtheory [44]) that only economies having technological origins are deserving of consideration and his populist conviction that the supplanting of "competitive market forces," however feeble these forces may be, by internal organization is anticompetitive.[45]

(3) Blake contends that there is now "hard evidence to support the . . . [theory] that large conglomerates facing each other in several markets tend to be less competitive in price than regional or smaller firms." [46] There are two problems with the argument. First, I would scarcely characterize the evidence on which Blake relies as "hard." Second, much of the evidence in question refers to geographically dispersed but relatively specialized multimarket organizations—which are surely horizontal rather than conglomerate structures—and hence is inapposite. Thus, although I share Blake's suspicions, at least with respect to the behavior of very large conglomerates,[47] the facts are still an open question.

(4) References to "mergers whose anticompetitive potential is so

widespread that it might appropriately be described as having an effect upon the economic system as a whole—in every line of commerce in every section of the country" [48] is unguarded. An understanding of the conglomerate phenomenon will be better promoted by delimiting the attack.

Blake's principal policy proposal is that conglomerate acquisitions by firms above a specified size (the subset of firms that are to be restricted is not explicitly identified, but Blake makes several references to the top 200 firms [49]) be accompanied by a spinoff of comparable assets.[50] He further stipulates that no toehold exception should be permitted. He argues in this connection that small, independent firms are more apt to engage in price competition than large conglomerates—relying a second time on the purportedly "hard" evidence referred to above—and contends that "a size based presumption would help restore the idea that internal growth is the normal, and usually the most socially efficient, means of industrial expansion, by making it the only means available to the largest corporations absent a special showing of procompetitive effect or of efficiencies." [51]

As already indicated, however, the evidence on which he relies is rather limited, and much of it inapposite. Moreover, the basis for his refusal to admit a toehold exception is really unclear. For one thing, the acquisition of a very small firm scarcely, by itself, contributes much to the growth of the large firm. Correspondingly, requiring the large firm to release assets in an equivalent amount whenever a toehold acquisition is made is scarcely more than a nuisance.[52] Furthermore, toehold acquisitions made for the purpose of securing a position that will subsequently be expanded *is* internal growth of the sort Blake favors. Either there is no point at all to Blake's toehold argument, or he regards internal growth by small firms as socially to be preferred to similar investments in large firms.

Assuming, arguendo, that the same investments will be made whether the small firm is acquired or not, it is easy to agree with Blake—though I repeat that the evidence on the competitive behavior of small firms as compared with operating divisions in large firms is scarcely dispositive. But it is doubtful that the same investments will actually occur. This raises transfer process issues.

An examination of these matters suggests that small firms apparently enjoy a comparative advantage at early and developmental stages of the technical innovation process.[53] Large, established firms, by contrast, display comparative advantages at the commercial production and distribution stages. Not only may the management of the small firm lack the financial resources to move to the commercial stage in any but a gradualist manner, since its credit standing does not permit it to raise significant blocks of capital except at adverse rates,[54] but the management of the small firm may be poorly suited to make the transition. Different management skills and knowledge are required to bring a project successfully to commercial development than may have been needed at earlier stages. If, because of management experience and team considerations similar to those described in 2.3 above, the talents needed to facilitate internal expansion cannot costlessly be identified and assembled, transferring the project to an established firm that already possesses the requisite talents may be more economical instead. Again, it is transactions, not technology, which dictate this result. Put in these terms, it is unclear that the no toehold position survives.

I am nevertheless sympathetic with the proposition that the acquisition of already large firms by other large firms ought to be accompanied by a divestiture of equivalent assets. For one thing, as Richard Hofstadter has observed, the support for antitrust rests less on a consensus among economists as to its efficiency-enhancing properties than it does on a political and moral judgment that power in the American economy should be diffused.[55] Since much of Blake's disenchantment with conglomerates appears to be attributable to a concern that giant size and political abuse are positively correlated,[56] I would urge that the case be made expressly in these terms. If giant firms rather than all conglomerates are the objectionable subset, attention ought properly to be restricted to these.

A requirement that very large firms divest themselves of equivalent assets when larger than toe-hold acquisitions are made is also favored by the prospect that this will serve to curb bureaucratic abuses associated with very large size. Although such divestitures sometimes occur voluntarily such efforts predictably encounter bureaucratic resistance. If, however, such divesture commonly has beneficial effects of an organizational self-renewal sort, making divestiture mandatory is scarcely objectionable. It merely strengthens the hand of those in the firm who are anxious to forestall bureaucratization. Absent such a rule, internal agreement on divestiture may be difficult to secure; parties with vested interests will make partisan (opportunistic) representations that will be difficult to reject. Given such a rule, however, the general office can simply plead that it has no choice but to divest (assuming, that is, that a large acquisition is to be made). The preferences of the general office, which reflect enterprise-wide efficiency considerations, thus are more fully made to prevail.

4. CONCLUSIONS

Kenneth Arrow has observed that "The identification of transaction costs in different contexts and under different systems of resource allocation should be a major item on the research agenda . . . of the theory of resource allocation in general." [57] The principal deficiency of received microtheory is precisely its systematic neglect of transaction costs in evaluating what, on self-conscious inspection, are plainly costly exchange relations.

As I would hope is clear from the above, neither vertical integration nor conglomerate organization can be accurately understood unless allowances for transaction costs are explicitly made. What is interesting, moreover, is that transaction cost considerations neither favor nor disfavor any particular organizational mode. Thus, while there are circumstances in which vertical integration predictably yields economies, there are other circumstances where it almost certainly will not, and still further conditions when it can have anticompetitive effects. Likewise, although the conglomerate can serve to energize competition in the capital market, whether it does turn crucially on organization form considerations—which is to say on the manner in which internal transactions are structured and managed.

Unfortunately, there does not exist a well-developed theoretical apparatus (in any sense comparable to that of received microtheory) for undertaking transaction cost studies. At its present primitive stage of development, the transaction cost approach is mainly an attitude, a way of looking at things. Whether the "institutional failures framework" that I favor, in which bounded rationality and opportunism are made to play a conspicuous role, or some alternative apparatus will be more fruitful instead is uncertain. Whatever the case, I would hope that my discussions in this paper concerning vertical integration and conglomerate organization demonstrate that the modern corporation constitutes one of the most interesting research contexts within which transaction cost investigations can be made.

NOTES

(Research for this paper has been supported by a grant from the National Science Foundation.)

1. For a much earlier call to take a transactional approach to economics—which, however, was not widely followed—see John R. Commons, *Institutional Economics,* Madison, Wis., 1934, Chap. 1. I do not mean to suggest that what Commons had in mind is identical with the approach employed here, but there are nevertheless similarities.
2. K. J. Arrow, "The Organization of Economic Activity: Issues Pertinent to the Choice of Market versus Nonmarket Allocation," in *The Analysis and Evaluation of Public Expenditures: the PPB System,* Vol. 1, Joint Economic Committee, U.S. Congress (1969), pp. 47-64.
3. J. E. Meade, *The Controlled Economy* (1971), Chaps. 9-11.
4. L. Hurwicz, "On Informationally Decentralized Systems," in C. B. McGuire and R. Radner, eds., *Decision and Organization* (1972), pp. 297-336.
5. H. A. Simon, *Administrative Behavior,* 2nd ed., New York, 1957. For a discussion of the limits of internal organization, see O. E. Williamson, "Limits of Internal Organization, with Special Reference to the Vertical Integration of Production," in A. Silberston and F. Seaton, eds., *Industrial Management: East and West* (New York, 1973), pp. 199-227.

6. E. Goffman, *Strategic Interaction* (Philadelphia, 1969).
7. This is merely a necessary but not a sufficient condition for internal organization to supplant the market. Internal organization also experiences distortion. Shifting a transaction from the market to a firm requires that a new efficiency gain be shown.
8. O. E. Williamson, "Market and Hierarchies: Some Elementary Considerations," *American Economic Review* 63 (May 1973), 316-325.
9. H. A. Simon, *Models of Man* (New York, 1957), p. 198.
10. In circumstances, however, where prices are sufficient statistics (in the sense of T. C. Koopman's discussion of a price system in *Three Essays on the State of Economic Science* [New York, 1957], pp. 41-54), reliance on the price system serves to economize on bounded rationality.
11. For a discussion, see O. E. Williamson, *Corporate Control and Business Behavior* (Englewood Cliffs, N.J., 1970), Chap. 8.
12. See Alfred Chandler, Jr., *Strategy and Structure* (1962); also Williamson, *ibid.*
13. This is not, however, to say that technological conditions and transactional factors (especially small numbers exchange relations) are independent.
14. For earlier, more extensive discussions of vertical and conglomerate organization on which the present paper relies, see O. E. Williamson, "The Vertical Integration of Production: Market Failure Considerations," *American Economic Review* 61 (May 1971), 112-125 and Williamson, *supra*, footnote 11, Chap. 9.
15. Arrow, *supra*, footnote 2, p. 48.
16. For any given level of output, the firm is committed to least-cost production. Assuming factor prices to be parameters, this entails equalizing factor price to marginal productivity ratios across all factors. But the firm is really interested not in minimizing costs but in maximizing profits, which requires that product demand considerations be introduced. Optimality is reached now when marginal-value products are set equal to respective factor prices. (The above ignores indivisibility conditions and corner solutions.)
17. Peter Diamond, "Political and Economic Evaluation of Social Effects and Externalities: Comment," in M. D. Imtrilligator (ed.), *Frontiers of Quantitative Economics* (Amsterdam, 1971), p. 31.
18. See Herbert Simon, *Models of Man* (New York, 1957), pp. 198-199.
19. G. J. Stigler, "The Division of Labor Is Limited by the Extent of the Market," *Journal of Political Economy* 59 (June 1951), 185-193.
20. *Ibid*, p. 188.

21. P. B. Doeringer and M. J. Piore, *Internal Labor Markets and Manpower Analysis* (Lexington, Mass., 1971), Chaps. 1-4.
22. *Supra,* footnote 19, p. 191.
23. R. Bork, "Vertical Integration and Competitive Processes," in J. Weston and S. Peltzman (eds.), *Public Policy Toward Mergers* (1969), p. 148.
24. W. Bowman, Jr., *Patent and Antitrust Law: A Legal and Economic Appraisal* (Chicago, 1973), p. 59. The ensuing discussion in this section follows my review of Bowman's book in the *Yale Law Journal.*
25. H. B. Malmgren, "Information, Expectations, and the Theory of the Firm," *Quarterly Journal of Economics* 75 (August 1961), 399-421.
26. F. M. Scherer, *Industrial Market Structure and Economic Performance* (Chicago, 1970), pp. 258-259.
27. The proposition in the text can be seen by examining Figure 14 in Bowman, *supra,* footnote 24, at p. 114. The vertically striped triangle in this figure represents additional revenue on sales between O and Q_m, while the horizontally striped triangle is the net revenue yield on sales between Q_m and Q_c. The social gain of perfect price discrimination, however, is given by the horizontally striped triangle alone. The proposition in the text then follows directly.
28. See Scherer, *supra,* footnote 26, pp. 254-255.
29. Bowman, *supra,* footnote 24, p. 115.
30. Variations on this argument apply, moreover, to an assessment of the welfare consequences of vertical market restrictions more generally.
31. The closest to such a position that I have discovered appears in the *President's Task Force on Productivity and Competition* (Commerce Clearing House, 1969), No. 419, pp. 28-42.
32. R. Solo, "New Maths and Old Sterilities," *Saturday Review* (January 22, 1972), pp. 47-48.
33. It is interesting in this connection to note that General Motors' executives went to considerable effort in the 1920s to apprise the business community at large of the character and importance of the multidivisional structure which it had devised, but to little avail.
34. See Chandler, *supra,* footnote 12.
35. R. H. Coase, "Industrial Organization: A Proposal for Research," in V. R. Fuchs (ed.), *Policy Issues and Research Opportunities in Industrial Organization* (New York, 1972), p. 67.
36. Williamson, *supra,* footnote 11, Chap. 9.
37. The appropriate kind has been designated elsewhere as M-form, type D_2; see O. E. Williamson and N. Bhargava, "Assessing and Classifying the Internal Structure and Control Apparatus of the Modern Corporation,"

in K. Cowling (ed.), *Market Structure and Corporate Behavior* (London, 1972), pp. 125-148.

38. A. Alchian and H. Demsetz interpret the conglomerate in a somewhat similar fashion. "Production, Information Costs, and Economic Organization," *American Economic Review* 62 (December 1972), 777-795. For a fascinating study of the use of the computer to extend the firm's capacity to deal effectively with a wider set of investment alternatives, see W. F. Hamilton and M. A. Moses, "An Optimization Model for Corporate Financial Planning," *Operations Research* 21 (May-June 1973), 677-692.

39. J. F. Weston and S. K. Mansinghka, "Tests of the Efficiency Performance of Conglomerate Firms," *Journal of Finance* 26 (September 1971), 709-722.

40. H. M. Blake, "Conglomerate Mergers and the Antitrust Laws," *Columbia Law Review,* 73 (March 1973), 555-593.

41. See M. Handler, "Twenty-Fourth Annual Antitrust Review," *Columbia Law Review* 72 (March 1972), 16.

42. Blake, *supra,* footnote 40, pp. 562-563, 572-573.

43. *Ibid.,* pp. 571-572, 574.

44. *Ibid.,* pp. 566, 578.

45. *Ibid.,* pp. 574, 579.

46. *Ibid.,* p. 570.

47. I would nevertheless caution that the conglomerate interdependence argument be used very sparingly. Recognized interdependence is easier to postulate than to operationalize.

48. Blake, *supra,* footnote 40, p. 567.

49. *Ibid.,* pp. 559-569.

50. *Ibid.,* p. 590.

51. *Ibid.,* pp. 590-591.

52. For size control purposes, a firm that engages in a series of toehold acquisitions within a specified time interval might be required to spin off assets comparable to the aggregate of those acquired.

53. A. F. Turner and O. E. Williamson, "Market Structure in Relation to Technical and Organizational Innovation," in J. B. Heath (ed.), *Proceedings of the International Conference on Monopolies, Mergers, and Restrictive Practices* (London, 1971), pp. 127-144.

54. Moving from a prototype to a commercial stage commonly involves a substantial investment in organizational infrastructure, much of which has no value should the enterprise fail. Lacking a known performance record and tangible assets to secure the investment, lenders, are apprehensive to invest except on a sequential basis. The risks of opportunism, given information impactedness, are perceived to be too great.

55. R. Hofstadter, "What Happened to the Antitrust Movement?" in E. Cheit (ed.), *The Business Establishment* (New York, 1964), pp. 113–151.

56. Blake, *supra,* footnote 40, pp. 574, 576, 578, 579, 591. That giant size procurs political favors does not imply that atomistic organization (e.g., the farmers) is the favored economic alternative. At least with the latter, however, the favors are apt to be out in the open.

57. Arrow, *supra,* footnote 2, p. 48.

FOUR

Power in America:
The Role of the
Large Corporation

Richard A. Posner

Professor of Law, University of Chicago

Professor, University of Chicago Law School. B.A., 1959, Yale; LL.B., 1962, Harvard. President, *Harvard Law Review.* Admitted: New York, 1963. Law clerk, Justice William J. Brennan, Jr., U.S. Supreme Court, 1962-63; legal assistant to commissioner, Federal Trade Commission, 1963-65; assistant to solicitor general, U.S. Department of Justice, 1965-67; general counsel, President's Task Force on Communications Policy, 1967-68; associate professor, Stanford, 1968-69; Professor, University of Chicago, since 1969. Subjects: Antitrust, (S); Natural Resources; *Regulated Industries,* (S); Torts; Trade Regulation, (S). Member, President's Task Force on Competition and Productivity, 1969; member, ABA Committee to Study the FTC, 1969; consultant, National Water Commission, since 1970; consultant, the RAND Corporation, since 1969; editor, the *Journal of Legal Studies,* since 1970.

The subject of this chapter is economic and political power—more specifically, the power of the nation's largest business firms—how great it is, how its exercise relates to our contemporary social problems, what (if anything) society should do about it. The continuing attacks in Congress and the press on the major oil companies and large corporations in other industries make this topic always timely.

BUSINESS POWER IN THE PERFECT COMPETITION MODEL

In the classical theory of perfect competition, the individual firm is a wholly benign and completely powerless mechanism for social wealth maximization. The preferences of the consumer are a given—the firm does not influence them. The prices that the firm must pay for its inputs (labor and capital) are also a given. Competition forces the firm to combine inputs in the most efficient way and to sell its product at a price just equal to its costs. This insures that throughout the economy resources will be used in a way that maximizes the ability of the economic system to satisfy consumer preferences, as determined by consumers' willingness to pay. The firm is *constrained* to operate in a way that maximizes its contribution to the social welfare. Should it step out of line—produce a different product from the one the consumer wants, or pay its workers a wage lower than they could get elsewhere, or charge consumers a higher price than other firms making the same product are charging—competition will eliminate it.[1]

All sorts of things that seem to be a part of the real world, or at least of the contemporary real world, are missing from the foregoing model. In this model firms do not monopolize; they do not seek to influence consumer preferences; they do not monopsonize (limit their purchases of inputs in order to depress the price of those inputs below the competitive level); they pay for all of the inputs they use; they operate at maximum efficiency (no slack); and they do not use the political process to advance their interests. What is useful about the model, however, is not its realism—I will stipulate that it is not realistic—but the fact that it affords a starting place for analyzing a complicated and ambiguous question, that of "corporate power." The firm in the world of perfect competition *is* powerless. By agreeing on that point we can proceed from a common premise. We can consider the implications, for the question of power, of complicatimg our simple model.

At least since Adam Smith it has been recognized that firms, if left alone, will have a propensity to monopolize, since a firm that charges monopoly prices is worth more to its owners than a firm that faces competition. At the time of the enactment of the Sherman Act in 1890 monopoly seems to have been rather widespread in America. In some industries most output was concentrated in the hands of a single firm—the Standard Oil Trust provided the outstanding example. In others the major sellers were organized into cartels that sought to eliminate price competition. The Sherman Act was interpreted as making cartels illegal per se and requiring the dissolution of Standard Oil and certain other single-firm monopolies. One can debate the precise effects of the Act and lament the inadequate resources, sanctions, and intelligence that have been applied to its enforcement. But it seems beyond debate that in the industries that have not been exempted from the Act overt cartels have disappeared though some covert price fixing continues, and that industries dominated by a single firm have become very rare.

It is possible to argue that in a market where a few firms account for most of the sales (automobiles, aluminum, cigarettes, and many others), prices will exceed competitive levels without any direct contacts among the firms of the sort that would subject them to punishment under the antitrust laws. The firms will collude "tacitly." This theory has some support in studies that have shown a correlation between concentration and profitability, although there are many puzzles and anomalies in these studies, and the results are subject to conflicting interpretations —one being that the superior profitability of firms in concentrated industries may reflect merely a "concentration" in those industries of firms of superior efficiency.

But assume that tacit collusion *is* a significant element in the contemporary economy. The assumption has no clear-cut implications for a debate over corporate power. The problem is limited to a relatively few firms in a relatively small number of industries, although the industries are important ones. The problem is one of relative rather than of absolute size—a multibillion-dollar firm having a small market share in a hundred markets would have no power over price. And the problem —if it is a problem—is an essentially technical one to be solved by an extension of our existing antitrust policies.

MONOPSONY POWER

It used to be thought that monopoly had significance for macroeconomic phenomena such as business cycles and inflation. Few economists hold this belief today. Monopoly leads to a misallocation of resources among industries, but there is no reason to expect it to increase the general price level or affect aggregate demand.

The other side of the monopoly coin is monopsony, the practice of limiting the purchase of an input in order to depress its price below the competitive level. The phenomenon is popular among textbook writers but rare in practice. It used to be thought widespread in labor markets—perhaps it was—but unionization must surely have eliminated it. It can hardly be contended that many companies today are paying their workers less than the workers would command in a competitive market for their labor. The purpose of unionization is, of course, to get the union members higher wages than they would obtain in a market that was freely competitive both on the demand and on the supply sides.[2]

Unionization is important to my analysis in a quite different sense. It suggests that the use of the monopoly argument in the criticism of the corporation is essentially spurious, a makeweight. Unionization is a source of monopoly power, exempt from antitrust laws, with the same misallocative effects as business monopolies; likewise the minimum wage. The combined monopolistic effects of the labor antitrust exemption and the minimum wage are probably greater than those of cartels and monopolies in the industries subject to the Sherman Act. But the people who attack big business on monopoly grounds do not criticize the union exemption or the minimum wage. Their objections are to big business and not to monopolization as such. We have yet to uncover the reason for their objections.

IMPLICATIONS OF EXTERNALITIES

Let us now consider the allegation that firms often use inputs without paying for them. One of the inputs into a factory's production is the clothing of the people living near the factory which is soiled by the smoke that the factory emits. The factory will not pay for that input unless forced to do so by the legal system. (This assumes, but realistic-ally, that it is too costly for the factory to offer to sell clean air to its neighbors. If it could create a market in clean air, then, as with any other resource, it would use rather than sell the right to dirty the air only if the value of the right to it were greater than the value of the right to other users.) Because the costs of organizing markets in such resources as clean air, pure water, and uncongested routes are often prohibitive, we observe many instances in which firms use inputs for which they do not pay. The same is true of individuals—the driver who pollutes and congests, the homeowner whose untended lawn offends passers-by.

The problem is a general one in any economic system in which people and enterprises will not pay for the use of a resource unless the existence of legally protected property rights, or some other social mechanism, forces them to do so. The problem has nothing to do with the number of firms in the economy or with their relative or absolute size. There is no basis for thinking that the amount of air pollution would be less if there were 100 manufacturers of automobiles than if there were one—there might even be more. A perfectly competitive automobile industry would have no incentive to install air-pollution control devices in its automobiles, because such a device increases the cost of the automobile without increasing its value to the owner (the device does not increase noticeably the purity of the air that *he* breathes). Indeed, it would be commercial suicide for a member of a highly competitive automobile industry to install the device. It would increase his costs without increasing either the market value of his product or the costs of his competitors, so he could not raise his price to cover any part of the added cost. A monopolist, in contrast, could pass on a part of the increased cost to the consumer by raising his price.

DOES ADVERTISING CREATE BUSINESS POWER?

Another feature of the model of perfect competition that strikes many contemporary observers as naïve is the assumption that the tastes or preferences of the consumer are external to the firms that are selling to him. Advertising is a common selling device, and the content of advertising seems designed to alter and shape the consumer's tastes—to make him like a particular product or brand, or even a way of life. Firms presumably would not spend money on such advertising messages if they had no effect, from which it would seem to follow that the advertiser—Procter & Gamble, General Motors, or whoever—must be changing the tastes of the public, surely a significant, in fact insidious, form of power.

A leading economist of advertising, Phillip Nelson, has argued that the content of advertising *is* irrelevant—it is only the frequency of the advertising that counts and it conveys valuable information to the consumer concerning the market's acceptance of the brand being advertised.[3] I will not pursue the argument here. I will assume that the advertiser is seriously concerned with persuading the consumer—by logic, association, insinuation, or whatever—to buy his brand, or product, rather than something else. I will go much further and concede, without believing, that the advertiser is trying not only to convince the consumer that his preexisting preferences will be best served by buying the advertiser's product, but to change the consumer's taste to fit the advertiser's preexisting product choice. It does not follow that advertising *in the aggregate* will change tastes. Advertisers will be competing with one another for the consumer's dollars. One will advertise Scotch and another beer and another dietetic soft drinks and another Hawaii and another a savings account and another health foods and another shoe polish. The process of competition should result in the consumer's choosing the product and service mix that corresponds most closely to his underlying structure of tastes, values, preferences, Weltanschauung, etc. Of course, if there was no advertising, people mightn't know how many experiences, things, sensations there were to desire. In that sense advertising in the aggregate may affect behavior. But I do not think we can despise this effect. As Frank Knight used to say, there is no poverty like the poverty of wants.

The conventional rejoinder is that only advertising stimulates the appetite for things that can be bought, but this is incorrect: thrift institutions advertise the joy of deferred consumption. If it were true, it would be a trivial point because there are many other institutions in society that contribute to the formation of taste—schools, and churches, newspaper columnists, the government, and parents, to name a few—some of which, at least, seek to develop tastes for other things besides purely material consumption.

PROFIT MAXIMIZATION AND BUSINESS BEHAVIOR

Firms in the classical model are assumed to be cost minimizers. This is just the other side of the coin of profit maximization. Profits are greater the lower the cost of the product being sold, holding the quality of the product constant. Profit maximization and cost minimization seem compellingly realistic assumptions as applied to competitive markets. So long as at least one firm in a competitive market wishes to maximize its profits, the other firms in the market will have an incentive to do likewise, for if they allow their costs to rise above the costs of the firm that is trying to minimize its costs their sales will decline, quite possibly to zero.[4] The less concerned with or adept at minimizing costs a seller is, the smaller will be his role in the competitive market. Business gravitates to profit maximizers.

Thus the belief that many firms, especially large firms, are not profit maximizers is correlative to the belief that effective competition is wanting in many industries. But it is not at all clear that monopolists are not profit maximizers. There is no reason they shouldn't be: every dollar that the monopolist forgoes by failing to maximize profit is a dollar lost. The profits that the monopolist loses by failing to minimize costs represent pure loss to the monopolist.[5] He has every incentive to avoid that loss.

Dropping the assumption of profit maximization wreaks havoc with the other criticisms of corporate behavior. There is no longer a reason to believe that large firms behave like monopolists or take advantage of opportunities to use certain resources (such as clean air) without paying for them or try to force unwanted products down the consumer's throat. The critic of corporate power can't have it both ways—he can't accuse the corporation of all of the vices that assume that corporations seek to maximize profits and of all the vices, such as slackness, or yielding to unreasonable union demands, or overpaying executives, or failing to hire superior members of minority groups that stem precisely from failure to pursue the goal of profit maximization.

POLITICAL POWER AND SPECIAL INTERESTS

By far the most serious criticism leveled against the large corporation, I believe, is that it uses the political process to further private ends. Private monopolies and cartels are inherently fragile. The monopoly price induces new firms (and existing ones) to increase production of the monopolized product in order to obtain a share (or increase their existing share) of the monopoly profits, but in the process of increasing production the firms drive price back down to the competitive level. The self-destructive potential of monopolies and cartels can, however, be eliminated by the intervention of the government to limit the entry of new firms and the expansion of output by existing ones. Much legislation appears to be designed to do just this. A good example is the Interstate Commerce Act enacted in 1887 to regulate railroads. The Act forbade price discrimination by railroads and also forbade them to price other than in accordance with published price lists (tariffs). We now know that this legislation was intended to, and did, help the railroad cartels prevent their members from selling below the cartel price by granting discriminatory, and often secret, rebates.[6] The Civil Aeronautics Act appears to have been designed—or at least it has operated —as a method of giving governmental sanction and support to a cartel of airlines by limiting entry and price competition. These examples could be multiplied many times.

The fact that a great deal of legislation appears to be designed to protect firms against competition does not, in and of itself, prove that business has an undue or unhealthy influence on the political process. Such legislation might simply reflect a pervasive public ignorance of the advantages of competition compared with cartelization. However, economists and political scientists have developed a theory which lays this type of legislation at the door of the protected firms.[7] The theory holds, in brief, that a compact group each member of which stands to gain or lose substantially from proposed legislation will exercise a greater influence on the legislative process than a very diffuse group, each member of which stands to gain or lose very little from the legislation. The airline industry exemplifies the compact group; airline passengers, the diffuse. The gain to each airline from successful cartelization is presumably great, while the costs of organizing the airlines for effective campaign giving, lobbying, etc., must be relatively small since there are so few airlines to coordinate. In contrast, the loss to the average airline passenger for the higher rates resulting from cartelization is small, while the costs of organizing the passengers into an effective political interest group would be very great because there are so many of them. Hence we expect, in general, that the industry will be more effective than the consumer in shaping legislation to its ends. This may explain why so much legislation seems to sacrifice the consumer on the altar of corporate profitability.

The kind of analysis suggested in the last paragraph provides the basis for a serious criticism of our political system and, perhaps, more broadly, of the role which we allow "interest" groups" to play in shaping public policy. It does not suggest a basis for a criticism of large corporations as such. The subordination of consumer to producer interests in the production of legislation seems quite independent of the size of the individual firms involved. We observe as much protective legislation in small-business industries, such as agriculture, textiles, and trucking, as in large—perhaps more. We observe much protective legislation in industries where production is carried on by individuals rather than by firms—unionized trades and regulated professions such as medicine are important examples. Moreover, we observe that protective legislation is typically sought by the firms *and* by the workers in the industries involved.

CONGLOMERATE FIRMS AND POLITICAL POWER

That the condition of being a large firm is not itself sufficient to assure protective legislation is illustrated by the embattled condition of the conglomerate corporations. These very large firms were not able to ward off highly adverse accounting and antitrust developments, or to preserve the market value of their stock in the stock-market decline of 1969-70. These values have yet to recover. Because conglomerates are by hypothesis highly diversified, they do not have common economic interests, and they have many natural enemies in the form of competing firms and firms that are possible targets for takeover bids by conglomerates. And within each conglomerate firm there are divergent interests that limit its ability to procure favorable legislation—for example, high tariffs might help one branch of the enterprise but hurt others that relied on imported inputs.

The conglomerates occupy much the same place in public rhetoric over corporate abuse today that the great monopolies of the turn of the century, such as Standard Oil, occupied in the muckraking journalism of their day. The political power of both groups proved to be weak, or at most transient. The trusts were dismembered, and the conglomerates have been buffeted from a variety of directions without obtaining any succor from the legislative branch.

The reason for the relative impotence of the large firm *as such* in the political process is, I think, the importance of numbers in that process. Interests groups are not effective unless they can deliver votes, either a great number of votes or a smaller number strategically concentrated in the close state or district. This means that the number of people who stand to benefit from protective legislation is critically important. That number is independent of the relative, or even of the absolute, size of the firm. If an industry has a million workers, it may well be a detail whether there are two or fifty firms in the industry. To be sure, the smaller the number of firms, the lower the costs of organizing them to operate as an effective political interest group; but the cost effect may be small in relation to the political clout that the number of employees contributes; and, to repeat, that number is unaffected by the number of firms. As for absolute size, a firm might have five million employees, but if they were in different industries (the firm is diversified), they will be affected differentially by any particular legislative policy that the firm seeks. If, to repeat an earlier example, the firm plumps for high tariffs to protect one of its branches from foreign competition, another branch may suffer because it depends on imported inputs whose price will rise if tariffs are imposed.

CONJECTURES ON THE THEORY OF CORPORATE ABUSE

I have canvassed a number of theories that attribute to the giant firm a malevolent influence on economic and social welfare. The theories are not impressive. This assessment would count for little if there were substantial—perhaps if there were any—evidence to support the theories. But there seems to be none. Every time an assertion about corporate power is investigated by means of the standard methods of social science research—a recent example is Professor Weston's analysis of the effects of industrial concentration on inflation [8]—the assertion is found to be unsupported. It is, of course, not surprising that illogical and inconsistent theories should yield predictions that, when tested empirically, prove false.

The remaining question, and a baffling one, is why an incoherent and unsupported theory of corporate abuse should command such widespread adherence, not only among ordinary people, but also, perhaps especially, among intellectuals. I offer the following conjectures—they are, I emphasize, no more than that.

First, ignorance about the nature and operation of a market system of allocating resources is apparently pervasive, even among supposedly educated people and even among ostensible experts (such as journalists writing about economic matters). The public reaction to the recent oil shortage is telling evidence of that point. Some of the most elementary propositions of economics—that demand is inversely related to price and that shortages yield above-average profits to suppliers—seem to be implicitly rejected by most people. Perhaps not one person in fifty understands the social function of profits, or that there is any.

Second, some groups have a vested interest in disparaging the operation of the market. One consists of people in government. They do not like to accept blame for economic problems created by foolish government programs, such as price controls and inflationary monetary policies and ill-conceived programs for regulating or subsidizing particular activities, so they try to convince the electorate that the real blame for economic troubles lies with greedy and shortsighted businessmen, union leaders, and other members of the private sector. Another group with a vested interest in disparaging the market consists of people who batten on the growth of government and attempt to justify further growth on the basis of the failures of private enterprise. Many people in universities and many lawyers are found in this group.

And here I think lies the essential clue to the hostility of intellectuals to free markets. In a free market, preferences are weighted by willingness to pay rather than by some intrinsic nonpecuniary worth of the preference. The hard hat's taste for Mickey Spillane has the same status in the market as the intellectual's taste for Jean Genet. Intellectuals do not like this democratization of preferences. They believe that their preferences are superior to ordinary people's, being the product of superior education, intelligence, and sophistication. They want to impose their preferences on the society, which requires the displacement of a market system of resource allocation by some form of central planning in which people like themselves make the major allocative decisions. The market system stands in their way, so naturally they dislike it.

Intellectuals are not the only people who dislike corporations. Working-class people tend to dislike business and businessmen too. It is quite natural to dislike someone who is your boss and earns ten times as much as you, especially if you do not understand the social function of the wage difference. But in our country the ordinary person's dislike of big business is in the nature of grousing, and he does not support radical measures aimed at destroying the market system.

Third, there appears to be an abiding public need to believe in the existence of invisible, global, omnipotent, indescribably sinister forces—Satan, Freemasonry, Papism, the Jews, and now the multinational corporations. The last satisfies the traditional requirements of a Sinister Force—worldwide in scope, mysterious in its modes of exerting influence, huge and monied. The multinational corporation, and its domestic cousin the conglomerate, have enabled the critics of business and the market economy to invoke and exploit the primitive emotional needs that unite us to our ancestors whom we deride for their superstitions.

NOTES

1. The mechanism by which competition eliminates the inefficient firm is not completely obvious and is discussed further in note 4, *infra*.
2. I am not making an argument for "countervailing power." The fact that unions attempt to obtain monopoly wages for their members is neither an efficient response to the monopsony power, if any, of employers ("bilateral monopoly" does not promote efficiency), nor a consequence of monopsony. The incentive to monopolize exists independent of whether one is dealing with monopsonistic purchasers.
3. See Phillip Nelson, "Information and Consumer Behavior," 78 *J. Pol. Econ.* 311 (1970), and "Advertising as Information," *J. Pol. Econ.* (forthcoming).
4. To be sure, a competitive firm, if it has an upward-sloping marginal cost curve, can, by reducing its input, continue to sell at a price equal to marginal cost, even though its marginal cost curve is higher than its competitors' marginal cost curves and even though it cannot raise its price without the quantity demanded of its output falling to zero. How-

ever, the result of the reduced output and higher marginal costs will be to reduce the rents received by suppliers to the firm, and these suppliers will respond by shifting the scarce resource that generates these rents to another firm (the landowner will rent his land to a more efficient firm in order to maximize the rent of his land). Thus, unless the owners of the firm are also the suppliers of the inputs that command rent, they cannot continue in business if they fail to minimize their costs. (If there are not inputs commanding rent, the firm's marginal cost curve will be horizontal and coincide with its demand curve, and an increase in its marginal costs relative to those of competing firms will drive it out of business forthwith.)

5. This is especially clear where the monopolist is a corporation whose common stock is publicly traded. Expected monopoly profits will be capitalized into the price of the stock, and any failure to realize the expected profits will lead to a reduction in that price and to an unequivocal loss for any stockholder who purchased the stock after the expected monopoly profits were capitalized.

6. See George W. Hilton, "The Consistency of the Interstate Commerce Act," 9 *J. Law & Econ.* 87 (1966); Gabriel Kolko, *Railroads and Regulation, 1877-1916* (1965); Paul W. MacAvoy, *The Economic Effects of Regulation: The Truck-Line Railroad Cartels and the Interstate Commerce Commission Before 1965* (1965).

7. See George J. Stigler, "The Theory of Economic Regulation," 3 *Bell J. Econ. & Management Sci.* 3 (1971); Richard A. Posner, "Theories of Economic Regulation," forthcoming in *Bell J. Econ. & Management Sci.*

8. Forthcoming in a volume on *Industrial Concentration: The Economic Issues,* H. Goldschmid, H. M. Mann, J. F. Weston, eds. (Boston: Little, Brown & Co., 1975).

FIVE

Some Financial Dilemmas

of the

Multinational Enterprise *

Sidney M. Robbins

Professor of Finance, Columbia University

and

Robert B. Stobaugh

Professor of Business Administration, Harvard University

Sidney M. Robbins
Professor of Finance, Columbia University (1957). B.S., 1932;
M.B.A., 1933; Ph.D., 1943. Finance, securities markets.
Consultant to various institutions including IBM, Abbott Labora-
tories, and the International Finance Corp.; board of directors and
chairman of Study Committee of the Oppenheimer Funds; member

* Much of this paper based on our book, *Money in the Multinational Enterprise: A
Study in Financial Policy* (New York: Basic Books, 1973). The Ford Foundation and the
Harvard Business School Division of Research provided financial assistance for the
research on which the book is based.

Advisory Board, superintendent of banking, New York State (we just issued major report that set the basis for new legislation being proposed). Just returned from serving as financial adviser to Central Bank of Vietnam. Served in similar capacities to number of developing countries throughout the world. Author of various books and articles in professional journals. Most recent is a book *Money in the Multinational Enterprise* (co-authored with Professor Stobaugh of Harvard University).

Previously served as chief economist for SEC Special Study Securities Markets; Consultant to various U.S. government agencies and other corporations; professor of finance and chairman of Department of Finance, University of Toledo.

Robert B. Stobaugh

Professor of Business Administration, Harvard University (1967). B.S., 1947; D.B.A., 1968. International business; management-production management. Coordinator, Harvard Business School Energy Project.

Other Publications: Three books and over 60 articles. Advisor to Federal Government: Alternate Member of President Johnson's Advisory Committee on Trade Policy, 1968; Consultant on Petrochemicals to President Nixon's Cabinet Task Force on Oil Import Control, 1970; Consultant on Petrochemicals to Office of Emergency Preparedness, 1971; Consultant to Department of Commerce, 1971 to present; Member, Advisory Council of Overseas Private Investment Corporation, 1972 to present. Professional Activities: Vice President, Academy of International Business, 1973-1974; Editorial Board of *The Journal of International Business Studies,* 1970-1972.

The big corporation has been on the economic scene for a long time; the big corporation with international ties is not new. But the emergence of a handful of corporate giants, with manufacturing facilities spread over a number of different countries, guided by a central management that thinks globally, is of relatively recent vintage.

AN OVERVIEW OF THE MULTINATIONAL ENTERPRISE

To put the multinational enterprise into perspective, let us cite a few figures. Foreign direct investment, mostly by multinational enterprises,[1] has been growing faster than either world production or world trades. From 1950 to 1970, the output of facilities owned by all foreign direct investors grew at an annual rate of 10 percent, compared with annual growth rates of slightly less than 8 percent for the gross national products and slightly more than 8 percent for the trade of the non-Communist world. As a result, by 1970 this output was 6 percent of the combined gross national products of the non-Communist countries and about equal to their total trade.[2] About half of all foreign direct investment is made by American companies. In 1973 the book value of this investment passed the $100 billion mark, and the market value was substantially higher.

The ties that hold together the broadly dispersed empire of a large multinational enterprise are strong. Like the nation-state, such an enterprise has a common language but it is expressed in the terminology of the accountant which is the same regardless of geographic location. Profits denominated in the currency of the home country represent a common standard and provide a driving objective whether the measuring unit is a dollar, lire, pound, or yen. And there is a sort of corporate nationalism manifest in the loyalty of the organization of employees in Europe, Asia, or the Americas. While it is hard to gauge the depth of this feeling, its presence can be sensed in the attitudes of local managements of overseas subsidiaries throughout the world. The flags of the multinational enterprises do not fly in the veranda of the United Nations, but their weight undoubtedly is felt in its inner chambers whenever international economic policies are under review.

OPPOSING TENDENCIES AFFECTING FINANCIAL PRACTICES

The multinational enterprise has been a great equalizing force in the transfer of industrial knowledge. For example, take financial practices. The parent is concerned with exposing its subsidiaries to new techniques of financial management and competition extends these practices to local firms. The parent spreads the gospel of the financial institutions with which it is familiar in the home scene, and eventually they dot the foreign economic landscape. As an illustration, the influence of U.S. firms has abetted the gradual transformation of specialized industrial development banks, originally formed in less developed countries to give financial aid to incipient industries, into traditional investment banks, serving as intermediaries between an emerging but still not very perceptive class of savers and fund-seeking enterprises; the U.S. experience also is apparent in the fostering of regional capital markets to help local concerns, as well as the expanding overseas operations of multinational firms.

Conversely, as overseas units follow foreign practices of relying upon commercial banks for much of their financing, the experience is reflected in a greater willingness on the part of the multinational parent to use commercial banks in the United States, particularly as the domestic capital markets run into foul weather. This tendency encourages the inclination of U.S. banks to spread their financing operations and eventually may pave the way for them to become members, through the holding-company veil, of the nascent central securities market in the United States. Behind these changes is the influence of the multinational enterprise which brings pressure for the creation of financial institutions in one country that were found helpful in its operations in another country.

In the long run, therefore, the multinational enterprise will be a cogent factor in the homogenization of the financial practices of firms throughout the world and of the financial institutions with which these firms deal. Accordingly, in some future millennium, when political giants have created a structure of world unity that ousts national jealousies; when economic giants have carved a system of stable monetary relationships; when fiscal giants have metamorphosed numerous local tax complexitites into simple international patterns—the financial problems encountered by the wholly domestic firm will be the same as those of the multinational firm. It is probably stargazing, however, to expect these varied giants to appear, at least in the foreseeable future.

For the present, therefore, the multinational enterprise must cope with currency values that change, national tax provisions that can be exploited, environmental factors that are dissimilar, and governments that at the same time offer the carrot of economic incentives while they wield the rod of currency and trade restrictions. So long as these conditions prevail, the perplexities and difficulties of officials seeking to manage the financial operations of their overseas units will remain unique to international business. Sure, there are similarities in that both the domestic and multinational financial manager may use comparable techniques in reaching financing, investment, or asset-handling decisions. This notion of sameness, however, is superficial. It sometimes has led to the dangerous practice of simply extending the role of the financial vice-president of a company that had been engaged primarily in domestic business to absorb the financial responsibilities of its swelling offshore activities. Such a policy is likely to produce a brutal learning experience. It is with an assessment of some of the managerial dilemmas created by the financial problems unique to multinationality that we now turn our attention.

THE CHALLENGES CREATED BY THE FINANCIAL SYSTEM

Several years ago, we undertook a major study of the financial practices of multinational enterprises, employing size and distribution of affiliated units as the major criteria of our definition of this term.[3] There were 187 firms that met our standards. As a rough average, each had some 40 overseas affiliates, located in at least 6 and in some cases over 100 countries.

A fundamental theme emerging from this study is that the multinational enterprise is a system that performs best when its management is aware of the opportunities growing out of the financial ties that link the system together. To take advantage of these opportunities, management commands a common pool of resources that can be moved through the system-binding links from one unit to another in accordance with a common strategy.

These financial links are represented by the different mechanisms for shuttling funds among the various units of the system. The most commonly used financial means of effecting such transfers include: dividends, payments for goods purchased, loans, principal reimbursements, interest on loans and accounts payable, fees for services and knowhow, and deferring or accelerating collection of receivables that have fallen due. Difficulties abound in the use of these links. Limitations may be imposed by the numerous governments involved. Logical courses of action may be obscured by complications inherent in efforts to coordinate the use of financial links and to employ one unit as a conduit for another. Determining both the choice of links and the direction of flows may demand unusual financial dexterity to take into account shifts in operating conditions.

Take the case of a major corporation, for example, that at one time financed, through deferred credits, the export of parts of a Brazilian assembly plant. Subsequently, the company changed its production scheme in Brazil to manufacture parts that were financed through local sources. Still later, the Brazilian unit began to ship the parts it manufactured to the parent in the United States which now helped finance these shipments by accelerated payments. All that remained steadfast in this instance was the location of the physical facility. As the nature of production changed, the pattern of financing was substantially rearranged. At the outset, the parent assumed the financing burden through delaying collection of receivables due it; then the subsidiary took on the responsibility of financing itself; and finally the parent resumed its financing character, this time by speeding payment to the subsidiary.

On top of these difficulties is the uncertainty created by the volume of choices involved which mounts dramatically as an enterprise grows. Thus, a single system consisting of a parent with two subsidiaries, each connected by ten different types of financial links, has thirty links all told. On the other hand, a relatively unpretentious system, consisting of a parent and twenty-four subsidiaries, with ten links between each pair of units, has three thousand intercompany financial links. For such a system, the number of alternative solutions would run into trillions—quite an intellectual chore for management to handle. Accordingly, it seems to us that the overriding financial need of the multinational enterprise is to recognize the enormous benefits that can be achieved through exploiting the system concept, while the accompanying financial dilemma is how to achieve this objective.Our analysis suggests that, by and large, enterprises have reacted in three primary fashions to this challenge, depending primarily upon their size and experience abroad. We also found after studying a half-dozen explanatory variables, that these characteristics were best captured by the enterprise's total foreign sales.

LEARNING TO USE THE FINANCIAL SYSTEM

Early in a firm's overseas advance, its headquarters management is dismayed by the steady panorama of problems that are unfolding but is not yet fully appreciative of the considerable advantages lurking in this development. The staff assigned to deal with the offshore business is small and has neither the time nor the background to cope with the surfacing new issues. As a result, the headquarters management avoids the job of directing the movement of funds through the company's financial links, even though the system is sufficiently simple to permit such centralized control. Rather, management allows each subsidiary to conduct its affairs with relative independence, a method of operation that is typified by the colloquialism "Every tub on its own bottom." The enterprise in this phase is comparatively small, at least by multinational standards, having foreign operations with less than $100 million sales in 1969.

The growth rate of these foreign operations is likely to outstrip that of the domestic area, and, as their contribution to overall earnings mounts, headquarters is encouraged to give attention to their management. The addition to the system of subsidiaries that engage in transactions with each other as well as with the parent creates more intercompany financial connections that, in turn, provide enhanced profit opportunities. An increasing awareness of this potential leads to the establishment at headquarters of a group of financial specialists and at the subsidiaries of a cadre of experienced financial managers. In the course of these developments, some type of shock may occur, such as a heavy inventory loss or a particularly inept currency transaction. Headquarters' reaction to such a disconcerting incident, when its foreign business has attained some critical size, is likely to be a decision to strengthen the central staff's ability to direct the financial aspects of foreign operations. Of the multinational group, it is the medium enterprise, with the offshore sales of about $100-$500 million in 1969, that occupies this organization slot, enabling it to exploit with relative effectiveness the system's latent earnings possibilities.

Eventually, the sheer intricacies of the foreign apparatus blur the competence of the headquarters group to map out in detail the financial relationships among the affiliates in its system. Accordingly, the method of handling the finance function now moves to the third phase which we have labeled "compromising with complexity." In this arrangement, the headquarters group formulates a "rule book" that provides standards to govern practices in such areas as local financing, inventory levels, and payment terms on intercompany accounts. Decisions on implementing these guideposts are left to the subsidiaries, while headquarters spends its time revising the rule book and reviewing only the major financial decisions of the subsidiaries and the results of their operations.

These observations about the practices of multinational enterprises are based on the analysis of interviews conducted with officials of a number of such enterprises as well as on an examination of extensive records that were made available to us. We also devised a computer model of a multinational system composed of a parent and two subsidiaries, one located in an economic environment characteristic of a developed country and the other in the environment of a less-developed country.[4] Although a very simple system, it is set up to simulate conditions in a real-life enterprise and has enabled us to gain some insights into the effects of alternative financial policies. For example, the model was used to assess the outcomes of the "arms-length" financial policy of the "small" enterprise, the "rule-making" policy of the "large" enterprise, and the "optimal" policy of the "medium" enterprise. As might be expected, the lowest consolidated profits after taxes were recorded when the units operated on an arm's-length basis; profits were lifted some 8 percent by the rule-maker and still another 8 percent by the system optimizer.

Only about one-third of the multinational enterprises we studied pursued optimizing tactics. Accordingly, the typical firm has considerable room to improve. For the small company, this means accelerating the learning process, for the big firm, it means shifting to greater reliance upon individualized rather than rule-making decisions. Through organizational changes, training programs, and extended computer analyses, the multinational enterprise is moving in this direction, but the pace is slow both because of the inherent difficulty in effecting adjustments and the jarring effects of resolving presumed differences between the interests of the corporation and of local governments.

THE BENT MEASURING STICK [5]

Accomplishment must be set against purpose. Thus, as a simple illustration, speed is a reasonable means of determining the performance of a racing car, but it is hardly an appropriate way of evaluating a vehicle designed for difficult travel. Similarly, management should assess the performance of a subsidiary in the light of the reasons for its establishment. Unfortunately, in the international area, these reasons tend to be overlooked because of the peculiarities of the individual case and the passage of time. It is conceivable, therefore, that headquarters may use a speed-type test to assess the performance of a subsidiary intended to operate in a difficult environment. In these circumstances, the measuring stick is bent.

Primarily, the managements of multinational enterprises establish overseas ventures as part of a strategic scheme. There may be a mixture of motivations at work. For example, a local plant may be necessary to reach a market otherwise blocked by tariff barriers; the intent may be to keep out, or keep pace with, a competitor; and the subsidiary may be the means of collecting and sifting information that facilitates planning in headquarters many miles away. Whatever are the underlying strategic considerations, they invariably involve heavy doses of personal judgment. Although the request to the board of directors, in deference to formal capital budgeting procedures, is likely to be couched in quantitative terms that could be quite elaborate, much of this paraphernalia may be gloss for a decision that already has been made. As an illustration, highlighted by contemporaneous developments, management may decide to participate in the exploration of a potentially giant oil field, even though the calculation of expected returns and costs indicate a loss, because the risk that a rival may uncover a major find, thereby improving its long-term competitive position, is too great to take.

As the years go by, the initiating strategy often is forgotten as the original decision-makers become preoccupied with other problems or are moved to different assignments. Perhaps more fundamental is the habit, ingrained from domestic experience, of applying an enterprise criterion, such as a designated return-on-investment, as the yardstick against which to measure performance. The real test of a subsidiary's contribution is the system results with and without its presence. But this is a hard concept to translate into numbers. The easy solution is to apply a familiar form of rate of return on investment as the basic measure of performance, even if the transfer-price mechanism is used to shift profits elsewhere in the system for tax or other reasons. The typical response of the bulk of the financial officers in our study was: "Our foreign subsidiaries are judged on precisely the same basis as our domestic subsidiaries."

In such evaluations, standard intercompany pricing and valuation figures often are used to report the profit or loss of the subsidiary without considering the offsetting advantages and detriments experienced by other units of the system in the results of the actual transactions that took place. Management's dilemma in this situation is how to judge the outcome of an investment that was made on the basis of marginal factors, whereas the ongoing results are based on average or standard figures. Moreover, economic conditions may vary widely from country to country; thus one subsidiary may face severe competition while another occupies a comfortable near-monopoly position. Added to these problems is the difficulty of making correct allocations to provide an understanding of actual cost-benefit relationships. Consider the case of a chemical company that introduces new products in the United States and brings to Europe only those deemed likely to succeed. The company charges its subsidiaries standard technical fees that do not take into account the burden of U.S. screening, thereby helping to promote the belief that its European operations are more profitable than those in the United States.

We have not come across any convenient technique to resolve this issue, but clearly it is desirable that management use the return-on-investment statistics of its foreign subsidiaries with discretion. To the extent possible, adjustments should be made to incorporate any effects flowing from the subsidiary's role in the enterprise system. Supplementary measures may be taken into account, such as growth in sales or share of market. Particularly important is the budget because it can be developed with attention to the circumstances distinctive to each subsidiary. In the meetings that are held between headquarters management and subsidiary representatives, these factors can be reviewed both in establishing original targets and in subsequent evaluations. As a basic maxim, it is probably safe to say that any effort to unravel the complexities of international operations is bound to place a high premium on the element of subjectivity.

THE MULTINATIONAL-CURRENCY GAME

How, for reporting purposes, a multinational corporation translates the numerous currencies of the countries in which its subsidiaries are located into the single currency of the home country is one continuing dilemma. The process could be dubbed the multinational-currency game, where the major objective is to avoid a translation loss and secondarily to report a gain. Which is shown depends primarily upon the mix of assets and liabilities held, and the desirable mix, in turn, depends upon the rules established by a referee, in this case an accounting authority.

Unfortunately, the multinational-currency game is not a pastime but a real-life activity in which corporate behavior is largely determined by accounting rules. The trouble is that not only are these rules subject to change and selection but their meaning is not clear. Recognizing this difficulty, one authority has gone so far as to assert that it cannot be resolved through a single set of rules or through alternative rules. He therefore proposes two methods, one for use by the parent company or other major equity investors, and the second by creditors of the company or other "outsiders." [6]

Whatever rules or sets of rules are prescribed, the likelihood is that they will have little economic meaning. The reason is that the economic effect of a devaluation or revaluation on a subsidiary's worth is difficult to foresee without a detailed understanding of the factors influencing the entries in the financial statements. For example, the devaluation of the currency of a country where a major subsidiary is located may cause a translation loss to appear in the consolidated statement. Yet, the devaluation could bring economic benefits to the system in various ways: changes in domestic pricing patterns may result in higher profit margins for the subsidiary; its export sales may be stimulated; other enterprise members may benefit by being able to acquire lower-cost components from the subsidiary in the affected country.

When a devaluation is on the offing, managers may take the necessary steps in accordance with the rules they observe to guard against a translation loss. Or, they could study the situation carefully and adopt the measures that appear to be in the best economic interests of the enterprise's entire system. Confronted with this choice, our experience has been that management invariably takes the accounting option for various reasons: it is easier, the translation loss represents a concrete quantity whereas the economic effects are uncertain; the translation loss may be interpreted as managerial ineptitude; or management may actually believe that the translation loss represents an economic loss. In part, the answer to this problem lies in the hands of the accountant who still has to provide well-defined translation guidelines; in part, too, it rests with management's understanding the implications of the rules and being willing to suppress the desire to follow them without taking into account the economic outcomes of the devaluation.

In addition to translation requirements, asset and liability adjustments because of expected currency swings are the outcomes of everyday business activity. In the course of buying or selling, financing, and providing or receiving services, a company constantly switches its debtor-creditor relationships. It then experiences a genuine loss when its financial managers, expecting a local devaluation, do not pay their debts denominated in other currencies. Subsequent to the devaluation, more local units must be converted into the other currencies in order to eliminate the same amount of debt.

Within the multinational system, as a protective measure, it is common for headquarters to order a subsidiary located in a shaky-currency country to pay immediately all intercompany accounts but to order the other affiliates to defer their payments to the subsidiary. From this defensive state of seeking to avoid a translation or conversion loss, it is only a step to move into the speculation arena where the emphasis is on seeking currency profits. Moreover, it may not be easy to tell whether a buildup of current assets in a strong-currency country is done for protective or speculative reasons. It is a bit like distinguishing between realism and prurience in art—the difference may lie in the eyes of the beholder.

NATION-STATE VERSUS MULTINATIONAL CORPORATE STATE

Like a domestic company, the multinational enterprise carries on the financial functions of raising funds, controlling costs, and managing assets and liabilities. Typically, therefore, the problems of both types of firms arising out of these activities are similar, although those of the multinational enterprise are often aggravated by the special conditions in which they operate. For example, while managers abroad are inclined to use the same inventory-control techniques that are employed in the United States, they must also cope with the added difficulties of ocean transportation, government export and import policies, and local custom. Unlike the domestic firm, however, the multinational enterprise is in a position to take advantage of differences among countries in the triad of currency relationships, interest costs, and tax rates. It is to be expected, therefore, that our multinational computer model would take these factors into account in seeking to optimize profits for its system.

Where the model struck off on an independent route was in its extensive use of intercompany financial links. In one period or another, it employed every link at its disposal to move funds within the system. As has been seen, the real-life multinational enterprise has trouble in coordinating the dispersed units of its system into an overall program that makes the best use of the interconnecting links and in judging how effectively its units contribute to the design of the program. While enterprises have adapted in different ways to the resolution of this issue, they are learning to recognize the benefits inherent in the systems approach and to move in the direction of conducting their activities in this manner. This tendency has significant implications for the future relationships between the multinational enterprises and the governments of the countries in which they operate.

At the close of 1971 the group of U.S. companies qualifying for our title of multinational had some $25 billion of cash or near-cash items and another $100 billion of inventory and accounts receivable held abroad that could be used as collateral to raise additional funds. The liquid assets of all non-American multinational enterprises were about of equal size. These huge resources far overshadow the central reserves of even the most powerful nations of the world and constitute a threat to their financial position. Except as a currency begins to totter, when visions of evaporating treasures cause panic reactions, our studies suggest that multinational enterprises do not move their funds in unison. This is scant comfort, however, to government officials who are aware of the increasing adroitness of multinational-company managers in shifting funds within their systems and of the considerable wealth of individual corporate giants. The rumbles of anxiety generated by these characteristics could readily turn into peals of concern that lead to the enactment of restrictive measures.

To the extent that foreign countries lose their comparative cost advantage and dismantle their barriers against U.S. exports, two of the important factors that have provided impetus to the rapid growth of U.S.-based multinational enterprises over the past quarter of a century will evaporate.[7] While the rate of growth may subside, we believe that expansion still will occur. Worldwide industrial progress is dependent upon the scientific and business technology disseminated by multinational enterprises through their sprawling networks of subsidiaries. There simply is no other economic entity in sight to take on this job in a world where markets are international and the key for entrance into these markets is such technology.

So, the scenario calls for continued growth of corporate multinational states that increasingly desire freedom to shuttle funds within the orbits of their own systems in order to tap the advantages of currency, tax, and interest differentials. On the opposite side of the stage are the nation-states ready to impose restrictions on these movements whenever they sense a threat to their financial position. When two antagonists are staring coldly at each other, the typical response is to restore cordial relations by the appointment of a referee who arbitrates the disagreements.

In the international area there are many overseeing bodies of both a political and an economic nature that function with varying degrees of effectiveness. Adding one more to monitor the activities of multinational corporations would follow a standard pattern, and discussions along these lines have been going on for some time in business, academic, and regulatory communities. Perhaps a new organization will come into being; it may even have a grandiose title like the "Group of Eminent Persons" created by the United Nations to study the possibilities of establishing some common rules to guide the activities of multinational enterprises. We are skeptical, however, about the feasibility of girding such an organization with any real powers because the self-interests of the competing parties are too well entrenched. The multinational enterprise is not eager to have another regulatory body with which to contend; the host governments are reluctant to surrender the right to control business firms operating within their domains; and, for that matter, the home country of the multinational enterprise is not likely to be happy about any encroachment upon its own authority by an outside party.

In these circumstances, our visualization of things to come in this area, at least over the foreseeable future, is for a new sphere of bargaining to open up between the multinational enterprise and the state. The enterprise will seek more permission to shift funds and will use as its bargaining lever the capital and technology that it could introduce into the country. The state will agree to a designated degree of mobility dependent upon its need for fresh supplies of capital and technology as well as upon its own economic position. Accordingly, in addition to his basic financial talents, the multinational executive of the future will have two important requirements: the ability to take the systems point of view in his planning, and the skill to negotiate with countries to obtain the necessary freedom to permit his planning to come into fruition. In this agreement, the nation-state has the political clout but the multinational corporate-state is the more efficient and enterprising instrumentality. Thus, we are witnessing the unfolding of an interesting confrontation between political and economic power.

NOTES

1. In direct investment an investor owns part or all of a foreign company and controls its operations. The definition of a multinational enterprise is quite arbitrary. For example, in order to obtain a list of U.S. firms to study, the Harvard Business School Multinational Enterprise Project arbitrarily took *Fortune* magazine's annual list of the 500 largest U.S. firms and selected those companies manufacturing in six or more foreign countries. The 187 U.S. firms that met these criteria account for about three-fourths of all U.S. foreign direct investment in manufacturing. See Raymond Vernon, *Sovereignty at Bay: The Multinational Spread of U.S. Enterprises* (New York: Basic Books, 1971), Chap. 1.
2. In this calculation the foreign output of the enterprise was placed on a "value added" basis for comparison with gross natural product but the total foreign output was used for comparison with trade flows.
3. Sidney M. Robbins and Robert B. Stobaugh, *Money in the Multinational Enterprise—A Study in Financial Policy*. (New York: Basic Books, 1973).

4. This model was constructed by Daniel M. Schydolowsky, professor of economics, Boston University.

5. For a more detailed discussion, see Sidney M. Robbins and Robert B. Stobaugh, "The Bent Measuring Stick for Foreign Subsidiaries," *Harvard Business Review* (September-October 1973), pp. 80-89.

6. Marvin M. Deupree, partner, Arthur Andersen & Co., "Translating Foreign Currency Financial Statements to U.S. Dollars," *Financial Executive* (October, 1972).

7. Sanford Rose, "Multinational Corporations in a Tough New World," *Fortune* (August 1973), p. 5.

PART III

The Corporate Economy
and Public Policy

The third and final section of this book deals with the corporate economy and public policy. Neil Jacoby provides a factual survey of the nature and dimensions of the corporate system in the United States. Michael Granfield examines the economic performance of concentrated industries and relates this performance to political attitudes about concentrated industries. Ronald Coase develops a framework for viewing public policy formation and a perspective for understanding the role of the economist in connection with the formulation of public policy.

Professor Jacoby begins with some of the basic factual information on business enterprise in the U.S. economy. He notes that there are more than five million established business enterprises in the United States. The ratio of enterprises to population has remained stable for more than half a century at about one firm for every forty people. More than eleven million Americans report income from self-employment on their income tax returns, thus indicating that in some sense there are eleven million entrepreneurial activities being carried on. Small business has held its own in terms of the number of firms and appears likely to continue to flourish in the service society of the future since service industries are characterized by small firms.

Professor Jacoby interprets these developments as indicative of underlying competition in the economy. He observes that contemporary competition should be seen as a dynamic process involving many dimensions in addition to price, such as product design and quality, services, warranties, credit terms, and trade-in allowances. Also, it includes rivalry between firms of one industry and those other industries for the discretionary income of the public, international competition from corporations in other countries, and potential competition from conglomerate companies ready to enter any market if profit prospects are bright. Tacit collusion among a few big firms in a market is unlikely because the decision variables are so numerous that no one company is able to predict the reactions of its rivals to any move it makes. Jacoby cited recent research findings that the returns to investment in big companies in concentrated industries tend toward the average, as one would expect when competition is effective.

Jacoby argues that the political power of big business has been greatly exaggerated. In fact, during recent years Congress passed a host of consumer protection and environmental laws in spite of business opposition. Federal regulatory agencies became tougher, and the courts piled new legal liabilities upon business. He states that corporate political power, which appears to have reached its zenith in the nineteenth century, has ebbed gradually over the years. Today, it is probably less than it has been since the 1930s.

Professor Jacoby interprets his findings to hold that the United States cannot appropriately be viewed as a corporate economy in the sense that big business corporations dominate American society. Corporate economic power, he argues, is effectively countervailed by the power of labor unions, farm organizations, professional societies, and a host of consumerist and environmentalist blocks. Social pluralism is on the rise. He concludes that our country has a heterogeneous economy with respect to the size and types of its enterprises, and that it is a pluralistic society with respect to the number and power of its different institutions.

This third part of the book is least balanced with regard to the range of evidence presented to the reader. But the counterarguments have been fully stated in the publication cited in the first note to Professor Jacoby's paper. These counterviews have been amply represented in literature and, in fact, dominate the public media. To some degree at least, therefore, the imbalance of this third section of the book may represent readdressing a previous imbalance in consideration of the issues and evidence involved.

Michael Granfield examines the concentration hypothesis, which is that concentrated industries are likely to engage in tacit collusion. He examines the condition for effective collusion under modern economic conditions and finds them extremely difficult to meet. He observes that price has many dimensions, that there are a host of nonprice factors such as quality, distribution service, warranty provisions, etc., which would have to be agreed on if a tacit understanding between firms were to be reached. He observes that the cost of enforcing any collusive agreement would be substantial and would likely exceed benefits, particularly since the potential gains from competing are very large.

Granfield argues that not only is tacit collusion unlikely on a priori grounds, but in addition statistical tests also provide counterevidence to the collusion hypothesis. He cites recent studies of the concentration-profit relationship. While some earlier studies have found a positive correlation, more recent studies have controverted these earlier findings. Later studies have indicated that the concentration-profit relationship dynamically changes over time. Any positive relationship at a point of time is likely to be eroded as firms of above-average profits trend down toward the average. Other studies indicate that the results are highly sensitive to the number of industries selected for the sample and the number of firms studied for each industry. Furthermore, multiple regression studies indicate that many other influences beside concentration may have a more important impact on profits. Finally, a size stratification reveals that the largest firms have higher profit rates in concentrated industries. But the theory of collusion would imply that firms of all sizes would benefit from the alleged tacit collusion that takes place in concentrated industries.

Despite the lack of empirical evidence to support it, the concentration hypothesis continues to hold wide popular appeal. From an economic standpoint, Professor Granfield observes that there is no basis in economic theory for establishing that an industry will perform better if it is an oligopoly composed of ten firms versus eight or six or of four firms rather than two. There is no basis for establishing that the performance of an industry with eight or nine firms is superior to the performance of an industry in which four or five firms account for 40 percent or more of industry output. The same argument could be made for augmenting small numbers by two or three additional firms.

Granfield argues that it is in the political area that an explanation for the popularity of the concentration hypothesis is to be found. It is the political ramifications of the issue that give it its appeal. Yet it is ironical that economic forces alone tend toward the operation of competitive forces and the achievement of competitive processes. The main interference with competition has been the size and values of the power of government to bestow monopoly privileges on individual groups and industries. He refers to the power of the government to confer this kind of protection as the "Monopoly, Inc. Store." He concludes that we must constantly seek to reduce the inventory of the "Monopoly, Inc. Store."

In his paper, Professor Coase continues the theme of the role of government in areas of economic policy. He begins with the question of whether economists have a contribution to make to public policy. He demonstrates that the observance of basic economic principles would constitute a substantial contribution to the improvement of public policy in the economic sphere. He points out that many important basic insights have long been known. The illustration he quotes would appear to describe many current situations if the setting were not specifically related to the period before 1776 when the *Wealth of Nations* was first published. Adam Smith describes the situation in which a shortage has developed. In a shortage, prices have an important role to play. A rise in price will diminish consumption and stimulate an increase in supply. But the displeasure of the populace with the resulting increases in prices leads the government to artificially hold down prices in order to prevent the businessman from increasing his profits. The consequence of government intervention is that it "exposes the people to suffer before the end . . . instead of the hardships of a dearth [shortage], the dreadful horrors of a famine." The irony is that with government intervention and the resulting aggravation of the problem, even greater blame is thrown on the businessman who appears to have controlled supply in order to increase his profits. The appearance of a shortage leads to government hearings as to why the shortage occurred and why the individual industry involved did not prevent the shortage. However, as government intervention aggravates the problem, there are no hearings on government policy as a major cause of transforming a "shortage into a famine."

To further illustrate how economic principles could make significant contributions if utilized, Coase cites similar observations by the British economist Edwin Cannon in connection with the use of price controls at the beginning of World War I. If there is an unusual rise in prices, people are generally convinced that the increase is "unnatural, artificial and wholly unjustifiable, being merely the wicked work of people who want to enrich themselves." Furthermore, when prices rise, people abuse the firms who are producing the product and whose increased production would cause prices to decline. It is of interest to note that Professor Cannon observed that "no amount of historical retrospect seems to be of much use. The same absurdity crops up generation after generation." These observations, made by economists over two hundred years ago and over sixty years ago, respectively, should provide some perspective on some current "shortages" in the United States and the world.

Thus, the economist has a useful role to play in tempering the short-run attitudes of people generally, and in pointing out the contributions that prices and profits perform in providing longer-run correctives to short-term problems. But the short-term immediate solution, of course, has greater political popularity and appeal. Nevertheless, bad policy creates much harm. But even ill-advised short-run solutions, Professor Coase observes, are a form of nonsense "subject to the universal law of demand: we demand less of it when the price [in terms of the harm it creates] is higher."

Professor Coase observes that some see hope in the development of the increased quantitative skills and factual information developed by economists. Such expertise may perform an increasingly important role in the development of public policy. Professor Coase, however, also emphasizes that nonquantitative economic analysis continues to be of great value. He observes that government laws and regulations are often wrong. Economic analysis can often predict in advance the undesirable consequences of specific government policies. In addition, quantitative empirical evidence can also establish the consequences of harmful government policies after the fact. To illustrate, he observes that when artificially low prices were set on natural gas by a government agency, it produced a government-induced natural gas "shortage." As another example, he cites the new drug relation procedures enacted into law in 1962. On economic analysis it could have been predicted that its consequences would be harmful to the public rather than beneficial. Empirically, it has been found that the number of new drugs introduced each year on the average in the period following the new drug regulations through 1972 was about 40 percent of what it had been in the prior decade, due to the new legislation. Both theory and empirical resulgs confirm that the gains from the exclusion of ineffective or harmful drugs were far outweighted by the benefits lost because of the delays in making available new, effective drugs.

Professor Coase concludes that government intervention is increasingly harmful rather than helpful because the government has been attempting to do too much. Because the government has been doing too many things, many of them are not being done efficiently. Thus, the problem is more one of big government than of big business. Hence, in formulating policy for the future we need to continuously reassess critically the role of large-scale enterprise wherever it is found. Large-scale enterprise in a changing society needs to take into account the changed conditions of society, and involves a reassessment of the roles both of large business firms and of large government organizations as well.

SIX

Myths of the Corporate Economy

Neil H. Jacoby

Professor of Business Economics and Policy,
Graduate School of Management, UCLA

Now a professor of business economics and policy in the Graduate School of Management of UCLA, of which he was the founding dean, Neil H. Jacoby has combined the careers of scholar, administrator, and corporate director. Born in Canada, he holds a B.A. and an LL.D. degree in economics from the University of Chicago, where he later became professor of finance and vice-president. For the past twenty-five years he has been at UCLA. He served on President Eisenhower's Council of Economic Advisers, was U.S. representative in the Economic and Social Council of the United Nations, headed official missions to India, Laos, and Taiwan, and has been a member of the Pay Board. Jacoby was president of the American Finance Association in 1949, was on the Executive Committee of the American Finance Association in 1949, and was on the Executive Committee of the American Economic Association in 1963-66. He has been an organizer or director of several corporations, including one of the largest multinational firms.

He is author or coauthor of more than fifteen books, including *United States Monetary Policy, United States Aid to Taiwan,* and *European Economics-East and West.* Jacoby is an associate of the Center for the Study of Democratic Institutions at Santa Barbara and a frequent contributor to *The Center Magazine.* His book, *Corporate Power and Social Responsibility,* was published by Macmillan in August 1973.

Social scholars have formulated a model of the American economy known as "the corporate economy." This concept is now widely accepted, mainly by critics unfriendly to contemporary economic institutions, but also by some who are hospitable to the present system. The central concept is that giant business corporations dominate American economic and political life and continue to extend their power. Managers of big corporations, it is said, effectively control their social environments. They exercise power over the governments that are supposed to regulate them, over the employees who work for them, over the consumers that buy their products, and even over the stockholders and boards of directors who, in theory, own corporations and are supposed to direct them. Big businesses are alleged to be able to manipulate the behavior of other economic groups so that their executives can pursue their own goals of security, power, and profit. Giant corporations are held to be the model and prototype of business in the future. Medium and small firms are thought to be disappearing. Freedom of enterprise is viewed as a vestige of a vanished age.

Many social critics go further and identify big corporate business with American society. They contend that great companies so dominate the policy and the society as well as the economy of the United States that it is a "corporate state." In their view, giant companies have made all social institutions—governments, unions, households, churches, even universities—subservient to their purposes, and wield virtually untrammeled political as well as economic power. For these critics, the errors and shortcomings of our society are those of big business; their social criticism coincides with their corporate criticism. A sampling of the writings of such social critics as Ralph Nader, Charles Reich, John Kenneth Galbraith, Andrew Hacker, Ronald Segal, Daniel Bell, and Willaim Lloyd Warner will demonstrate that I have not given an exaggerated account of the "corporate state" thesis.[1]

Because the "corporate economy" and "corporate state" theses are widely believed by the public and in the intellectual community, they deserve serious examination. My researches during recent years into the role of corporate business in the United States have led to the conclusion that these concepts are false and distorted caricatures of the true nature of the American economy and society. In truth, the U.S. economy continues to be heterogeneous and pluralistic with respect to the forms and sizes of its institutions, and is becoming even more so. Although the large business corporation is an important institution, the idea that giant corporations "dominate" our society is simplistic; and the notion that the United States has become a "corporate state" is pure myth. In presenting the evidence that supports these conclusions, I shall draw heavily upon my recent book, *Corporate Power and Social Responsibility*, as well as upon the work of my colleagues, much of which appears in a monograph, *The Impact of Large Firms on the U.S. Economy*, edited by Professors J. F. Weston and Stanley Ornstein.[2]

The "corporate economy" and "corporate state" theses can conveniently be factored into three major parts. First, they embody the idea that the present structure of enterprises in the United States is one of *great and increasing concentration*, that small business are disappearing, and that free enterprise is waning. Secondly, they encompass the belief that the corporate giants wield *great monopoly power* over the markets of the economy in which they acquire labor, capital, and materials and sell their products. Third, they encompass the notion that big businesses exercise *great political power* over the legislators, regulators, and other public officials with whom they deal. I shall call these, respectively, the myth of structural elephantiasis, the myth of monopoly power, and the myth of political omnipotence.

THE MYTH OF STRUCTURAL ELEPHANTIASIS

At the end of 1968 the United States contained about 1.6 million active profit-seeking corporations, one for each 125 persons in the human population. The corporate population grew rapidly after World

War II, at a rate about four times the growth rate of the human population. One reason was that more business proprietorships and partnerships incorporated to gain the benefits of limited liability, shelter for taxable income, and other advantages of the corporate form. Yet even in 1968, corporations formed less than one-third the total number of American business "enterprises," which was 5.1 million or one for every 40 persons in the human population. The "enterprise" population, defined to include all firms with at least one employee and an established place of business (but to exclude farming and professional services) has expanded *pari passu* with the human population. *The 1/40 ratio of enterprises to people has been constant for more than half a century.* The postwar growth of big firms has been accompanied by an unflagging expansion of the number of small firms—a phenomenon associated with the steady transformation of our nation from an industrial to a service economy.

The population of "enterprises" does not, however, provide a complete measure of the prevalence of entrepreneurship in the United States, because it excludes farmers, professionals, one-man firms, and people who do business out of their own homes. A conservative estimate of the entrepreneurial population is given by the number of individuals filing federal income tax returns reporting income from self-employment. More than 11 million persons did so for 1968, one for each 18 persons in the human population. This ratio, too, has not changed in the past quarter century. As large a proportion of working Americans now work for themselves as in 1945.

These facts contradict the notion that individual enterprise is waning in American society, or that freedom of enterprise has become an empty phrase.

Of course, the vast majority of enterprises are small, a minority are of medium size, and several hundred are large. The interesting questions concern the causes of the concentration of business in some industries in the hands of giant corporations; and whether concentration has been rising and is likely to rise in the future. The major basis for a widespread belief in rising business concentration is a study of the Federal Trade Commission, covering the years 1948 to 1967, which found that the "200 largest" U.S. manufacturing companies had raised their collective share of total manufacturing assets from 48 percent to 59 percent.[3] But careful analysis shows that this does *not* clearly prove that aggregate concentration in the U.S. economy has been rising. Dr. Betty Bock has properly observed that to select a *changing sample* of the "200 largest" firms year by year is necessarily to study a biased sample of the most rapidly growing companies.[4] She found that a *constant group* of the "200 largest" firms in 1954 held 51 percent of total manufacturing assets in that year and exactly the same percentage in 1968! There was no increasing concentration. She also found that the value added by an enterprise is a more valid measure of its economic importance than its total assets; and that by this criterion the share of total manufacturing business carried on by the "200 largest" companies was much less pronounced, rising from 37 percent to 42 percent between 1954 and 1967 and showing virtually no change after 1963. Professor Weston has shown, moreover, that most concentration in manufacturing was confined to six industries of very high capital intensity, in which enterprises of large scale are essential to realize economies of scale.[5] No less than 53 of the "100 largest" American corporations were in these capital-intensive industries—petroleum refining, motor vehicles, steel, industrial chemicals, nonferrous metals, and aircraft. The fact that these are also the industries of highest concentration in other industrialized nations indicates that common causal factors were at work. Finally, we should note that there is a constant turnover of about 1.6 percent per year in the composition of the "200 largest" corporations, as some firms come to the front and others drop out of top ranking.[6]

We may conclude that the evidence is ambiguous on the question whether there really was a significant postwar rise in *aggregate* industrial concentration in the United States. Even granting that there was a moderate increase, it was apparently motivated by efforts to realize economies of scale. More important, it was *not* accompanied by any increase in *market* concentration, which is more relevant to the existence of monopoly power.

There is also evidence that the relative profitability of big corporations has worsened in recent years. *Fortune* reports that the profit rates of the largest 500 U.S. industrial companies (the largest 500 in each year, not the same 500 over the whole period), which were higher than other industrial corporations up to 1965, fell below them in the period from 1965 to 1971. The relative decline in profitability of a *constant* 500 firms probably would have been even greater. Because business growth depends heavily upon profitability, this betokens slower future growth of the giants. Also, future economic expansion will be greatest in the service industries, in which medium and small firms predominate. Small companies occupy an enduring position in the U.S. economy, and it is a serious error to believe that they are destined to vanish. Concentration is unlikely to rise in the future.

If the "corporate economy" and "corporate state" theses were correct, one would expect to find that big firms in the corporate sector occupied a preponderant and increasing share of the economy. The truth is that the whole corporate sector has accounted for about half or less of the U.S. economy, depending upon which measure of its importance is used; and that its role has been relatively stable for a generation. In 1968 corporations generated 56 percent of the national income—the same share as in 1940. They employed less than half the labor force, and *large* corporations employed less than one-quarter of the labor force. Corporations own only 28 percent of the tangible wealth of the nation, about the same percentage they have owned for half a century. Corporations received rewards in the form of before-tax profits of about 10 percent of the national income—not much different from the percentage in 1940. Thus the facts do not support the thesis of galloping corporate elephantiasis. The real development has been *governmental* elephantiasis. Whereas the corporate sector has had a stable relation to the U.S. economy during the past quarter century, the governmental sector—measured by tax and other revenue—mounted from 24 percent to 34 percent of the GNP during the period 1950-70.

THE MYTH OF CORPORATE MONOPOLY POWER

The second count in the indictment brought by supporters of the "corporate economy" thesis is that big corporations possess great monopoly power. They reason as follows: *First,* concentration in many product markets served by large corporations is relatively high, when measured by the combined market shares of the leading four American firms. *Second*, high concentration of the industry causes the managers of the few leading firms to recognize the interdependency of their pricing and production decisions, and thus tacitly to maintain higher prices and profits, and lower sales, than would be made under effective competition. *Third*, this oligopolistic behavior brings idle capacity, excessive profits, and a loss of public welfare. *Fourth*, economies of scale do not require giant firms and existing high levels of concentration for maximum efficiency. The critics conclude that giant companies in concentrated industries should be broken up into smaller units and that mergers should be severely restricted.

Recent research into the nature of competition among large firms in concentrated industries leads to quite different conclusions from those reached by the conventional critics of big business. Factual evidence from the economies of many developed nations shows that large firms and relatively high concentration ratios in such industries as autos, steel, aluminum, or aircraft, have resulted from the intensive use of capital to realize the economies of enterprise scale, and that they are the product of competitive processes. It indicates that, when we take into account the expanding size of markets as a result of growing interregional and international competition, concentration is much lower than is usually perceived, and that it is diminishing through time. Most important, the true nature of competition among big firms in concentrated industries is now seen to be much different from the simple price-and-output adjustment process for a static "product" described in classical economic theory.

Contemporary competition is a dynamic process involving many variables. This multidimensional competition among the firms of an industry embraces rivalry not only in prices but also in product design and quality, services, warranties, credit terms, financing, trade-in allowances, and other factors. It embraces rivalry between the firms of one industry and those of other industries competing for a larger share of the supernumerary income of the public. It encompasses potential competition from new firms, ready to enter the industry if profit prospects appear favorable. And it engrosses international competition from firms in other countries, a rising number of which are involved in global operations.

The result is that even in concentrated industries, our market system on the whole produces an effective allocation of resources, normal profits, and a continual flow of new and improved products. Accordingly, blanket bans on mergers or wholesale corporate breakups would not serve the public interest. Instead, public policy should seek to stop or prevent specific acts of noncompetitive behavior. More important, it should seek to enlarge markets and reduce barriers to entry into all lines of business. A *positive* policy for competition is sorely needed, to augment our present negative approach.

In the perspective of dynamic multivectored competition, the economic power of the big corporation is seen to be limited by many forces, each of which appears to be rising through time.

(1) *Interindustry competition* for consumers' discretionary income is becoming more intense as the relative amount of such income rises. (Discretionary income is income not required to purchase conventional "necessities.") Thus, the critical decision for a consumer often is not which brand of auto to purchase, but whether to buy an auto, a vacation, a boat, a summer cottage, or a high-fidelity music system. Such interproduct competition puts pressure upon firms in many industries to keep prices down and to offer new or improved products in order to gain the favor of fickle and fancy-free customers. As Weston has noted, in an affluent society "product substitution may be the most severe and devastating form of competition." [7]

(2) *International competition* obviously continues to rise, as scores of foreign corporations have penetrated American markets since World War II. Twenty years ago, the American auto, steel, electrical, and electronic manufacturers had the domestic market to themselves. Today, the behavior of General Motors is disciplined by Volkswagen, Toyota, Datsun, Volvo, Fiat, as well as by Ford and Chrysler. The prices of U.S. Steel are tempered by those of Nippon Steel, by Mitsubishi and Thyssen as well as by those of Bethlehem and Youngstown. General Electric bids on turbines are held down by the actions of Siemens, English Electric, and Brown-Boveri as well as by those of Westinghouse. Indeed, where markets are international, the true concentration ratios are about half as large as those measuring the American market only.

(3) *Potential competition* is also a vector of increasing force, as the postwar movement toward corporate diversification has gained momentum. An increasing number of large companies, having both the

motive and the necessary resources, stand ready to enter any market where profit opportunities appear bright. Established firms in any industry cannot prudently ignore the probability that firms from many other industries will enter if they achieve high prices and high profits.

Traditional economic theory has tended to ignore or to minimize the influence of these many dimensions of the competitive process. But when we see contemporary competition among large firms as a multi-vectored dynamic process, it is readily understood why it is normally effective in reducing their market power and making it serve the public welfare. Tacit collusion is simply not feasible. Because the decision variables are so numerous, no producer is able to anticipate the precise reactions of his rivals (even if they are few) to competitive moves that he makes. Hence, one may concur with the conclusion reached by A. D. H. Kaplan some years ago, that the weight of evidence indicates the contemporary competition is generally effective and that it exerts a strong discipline upon the behavior of large corporations.[8] Indeed, as Kaplan observed, contemporary competition operates *more* powerfully than classical competition to serve consumers: "When compared with the improvement in performance that a consumer's dollar has been able to buy in drugs and gasoline, in sound reproducing machines, or in miracle drugs, the downward price pressure of atomistic competition appears relatively feeble."

The conclusion that contemporary competition is usually effective among large firms in concentrated industries finds empirical confirmation in recent research into the relation of concentration to profitability. If competition is effective in an industry, returns on investment in that industry should tend toward the average return over a period of time. Many past studies claimed to find that profit rates were higher in concentrated industries than in unconcentrated ones. However, recent studies by Professors Demsetz, Ornstein, and Weston at UCLA and by Professor Yale Brozen at the University of Chicago cast doubt upon the traditional view and indicate, instead, a tendency of investment returns to firms in concentrated industries to converge upon the average rate of return.[9] Such a finding suggests the presence of effective competition.

Recent research has also demonstrated the falseness of the notion that prices charged by big companies for their products have been more inflationary than other prices because of monopoly power. In fact, such prices have been less inflationary in their effects upon the Consumer Price Index. Another shibboleth has been that the prices charged by big corporations are more rigid and inflexible than other prices because sellers are able to "administer" them. Recent research has also shown this notion to be without foundation. Actual transaction prices (as distinguished from *quoted* prices) of the product of concentrated industries apparently have behaved much like other prices.[10]

In summary, recent empirical research into the behavior of large firms in concentrated industries tends to substantiate the view that competition is generally effective. Evidence is lacking that they act according to the older theories of oligopoly. The myth of corporate "shared monopoly" should now be consigned to the intellectual dustbin. Neither behaviorally or structurally does the United States have a "corporate economy."

THE MYTH OF CORPORATE POLITICAL OMNIPOTENCE

We come now to the third main argument in the "corporate economy" and "corporate state" theses—that corporate business wields great power over the political processes and organs of American government. Many believe that big business dominates elections through campaign contributions, controls legislation by lobbying, influences regulatory agencies by favors and promises of lucrative jobs, and even sways the courts.

Undoubtedly, the big corporation *does* endeavor to influence all phases of politics, as does the labor union, the farm organization, the American Medical Association, and many other institutions of our pluralistic society. To this end, it typically employs a variety of instruments. Its officers and directors contribute to the campaigns of political candidates. The firm joins trade and industry associations. It maintains a Washington representative. It has a public affairs department at its headquarters. It lends its executives for tours of duty in government. And it lobbies in the corridors of legislatures in behalf of laws that will lighten its burdens and expand its opportunities. The two basic questions are, however: Does the business corporation have a legal and moral *right* to seek to influence government? And, how *influential* has business actually been?

In responding to the first question, we should recall that the founders of our republic were individualists who sought to curb the authority of the state over the citizen. They designed a government of limited powers, divided into three branches, each checking and balancing the other. They wrote a Constitution guaranteeing the individual's right to associate freely with others. These factors, the federal structure of American government, and the ethnic diversity of our people encouraged the formation of all manner of private institutions to which the state delegated limited powers.

Thus arose our pluralistic society, composed of many institutions competing with each other for the attention and resources of the people, and for the favors of government. Trade union, farm association, school, church, professional guild, and corporation all vie for political influence. In this institutional competition it is expected that each social organ will be restrained by the actions of others. Countervailing political power will prevent a single institution from dominating the others and using government to foster its special interests over the public interest. The aim is to maintain a felicitous balance of power. Should a serious disproportion develop, balance can be restored by limiting the dominant institution, or by creating new countervailing political blocs to oppose it. Thus, President Franklin D. Roosevelt's New Deal in the 1930s powerfully encouraged the growth of labor and farm organizations to offset the political influence of corporate businesses.

The industrial pluralism of American society requires institutional politicization. If only to assure its survival, each institution is compelled to involve itself with government. Thus, the church must continually fight a political battle to maintain its exemptions from taxation. The labor union has its Washington lobby and its political action committee to elect representatives pledged to foster the interest of organized labor. The business corporation likewise has no choice but to be as politically influential as the law and its resources permit. Indeed, corporate political action is protected by the federal Constitution, the First Amendment which guarantees to all citizens the right to petition the government for a "redress of grievances." The salient issue thus is not whether corporations should engage in political activities but *how extensive* the corporate political role should be.

We shall not pause here to explore that important question. Instead, we shall try to measure the contemporary political base of corporate business. My studies have led to the same conclusion reached by Professor Edwin M. Epstein of our Berkeley campus. He wrote: "Corporate political power does not presently constitute a danger to the American pluralistic democracy, which continues to produce legislation, rulings, decisions and programs that are contrary to the desires of significant corporate interests." [11]

One way of measuring corporate political power would be to compile a year-by-year scorecard of the successes and failures of business to obtain from the Congress the kind of legislation it favored and to defeat those bills it opposed. A similar "scorecard" might be constructed for issues before the regulatory agencies and the courts. If business persistently scored many more successes than failures in all areas of politics, we might conclude that it did indeed possess formidable political power.

Unfortunately, such a scorecard cannot easily be completed. The main difficulty is to determine what *is* the "business interest." At any given time, corporations are split on most national issues. Thus, petroleum companies have opposed liberal oil import quotas, while petrochemical companies have favored them in order to obtain less expensive feedstocks. Steel companies have sought quotas upon imports of foreign steel, whereas auto companies and other large steel users have fought them. Even with respect to antipollution regulation, business often had no united front because of opposing interests. For example, deep coal mining companies in the East favor tough environmental statutes to control strip-mining companies in the West, because that will raise the cost of strip-mined coal and reduce its competitive advantage over the eastern coal.

Nevertheless, it is possible to identify a "business" stand on some important issues of recent years. American business finally did succeed in obtaining the realistic depreciation and the investment tax credits earlier found in most other developed nations. It did defeat labor union efforts to repeal the "right-to-work" provisions of the Taft-Hartley Act. On the other hand, business lost its battle against the Water Quality

Standards Act in 1965, the Air Quality Act in 1967, the Fair Packaging and Labeling Act in 1966, the Highway Safety and Motor Vehicle Safety Standards Acts in 1966, the Consumer Protection Act in 1968, and the Bituminous Coal Mining Health and Safety Act of 1970. A spate of consumerist and environmental legislation was passed against the opposition of most business organizations and of some of the largest corporations. This record suggests that, during recent years, business fought a defensive action against other interest groups in the Congress, and that it failed more often than not.

There is also abundant evidence that, during the 1960s, corporate business was generally unable to bend federal administrative agencies to their will—contrary to the popular notion that they have "captured" these agencies. The antitrust agencies laid down restrictive guidelines that have almost stopped vertical and horizontal mergers, and they filed many suits, especially against firms in concentrated industries and corporate conglomerates. The Federal Trade Commission promulgated tough new prohibitions against false and deceptive advertising. The Federal Power Commission continued, under strong protests, to hold down the wellhead price of natural gas. State public utility commissions held down electric rates in an era of inflation to the point that the ratio of market to book value of electric utilities stocks was cut in half during the last decade. The Federal Communications Commission tightened its requirements for the renewal of broadcasting licenses. The Securities and Exchange Commission compelled diversified companies to disclose their sales and profits by product line and deepened its inquiries into accounting and financial reporting practices.

All of these actions refute the idea that business has "captured its regulators." While most experts present at a conference convened by the Brookings Institution in 1971 agreed that "much of business regulation in the United States is in deep trouble," their consensus was that the causes went far beyond undue solicitude for business interests.[12]

Also, there has been a strong trend in judicial decisions during the past decade toward increasing the liabilities of business for the performance of products under warranty, for damage to third parties, and for pollution of air and water. The potential costs of such liabilities have been multiplied by the rising use of class-action suits, in which one person may sue in behalf of thousands of others who stand in the same relationship to a company. Stockholder suits alleging misbehavior by corporate officers and directors have multiplied, as SEC regulations have become stricter. This continuing judicial enlargement of business responsibilities reflects the influence of public opinion upon the courts. It demonstrates the weakness of corporate political influence.

Finally, the general acceptance of Keynesian fiscal policy must be mentioned. It led to the passage of the Employment Act of 1946 and to an active role for government in guiding economic activity. Prosperity became a *political* responsibility. The views of businessmen about economic affairs became less influential. Business dependence upon government deepened.

Thus, the weight of evidence supports a conclusion that corporate political influence upon government waned significantly during the 1960s and is not today a danger to American pluralistic democracy. Consumer-oriented political blocs have burgeoned. The Urban Coalition, Common Cause, Nader's "Raiders," the Sierra Club, and a host of other organizations now raise their voices in behalf of the common citizen. Their political potency was proved by their success in persuading Congress to enact a succession of measures for consumer and environmental protection. Corporate political power, which appears to have reached its zenith during the nineteenth century, has ebbed gradually over the years. Today, it is probably relatively less influential than it has been since the 1930s.

A HETEROGENEOUS ECONOMY IN A PLURALISTIC SOCIETY

The evidence shows that the United States is not now, and is not becoming, a "corporate economy" or a "corporate state" as these phrases have been used. It is now, and is likely to remain, a *heterogeneous economy* with respect to the types, sizes, and legal forms of its enterprises. Big corporations are not the prototypes of the future. Most Americans do not work for big corporations; most work for medium and small businesses, governments, and nonprofit institutions such as hospitals, foundations, and universities. Small business maintains its role in the economy.

Ours is a *pluralistic society,* not dominated or overwhelmed by any one institution; and this social pluralism is on the rise. Just as corporate economic power is effectively constrained, as a rule, by market competition, so is corporate political power effectively countervailed by the power of labor among farm organizations, professional societies, and a growing number of consumerist and environmentalist blocs. It is time to rid our minds of the myths of corporate elephantiasis and of corporate economic and political omnipotence.

To eliminate mythology is, however, only a first step toward understanding the true role of corporate business in our society. The next step must be to enlarge our knowledge of corporate performance and of corporate relationships with government and other social institutions. For that purpose, much more patient and objective research is required. Yet we already know enough, I believe, to propose salutory reforms. We should make the boards of directors of corporations more responsive to the changing needs of society. We should offer stronger incentives to business to clean up the environment and tackle other social problems. We should restructure government procurement processes for high-technology military hardware to make the corporation a more efficient supplier of the tools of national defense.[13] Indeed, we should take steps to make all of the major institutions of our evolving society function more effectively. Meanwhile, a fair assessment of the evidence entitles us to conclude that the big business corporation is a necessary and useful institution of our heterogeneous economy and pluralistic society.

NOTES

1. See the following works for examples: *America Incorporated: Who Owns and Operates the United States?* by Morton Mintz and Jerry S. Cohen (New York: Dial Press, 1971) Introduction, Prologue, and Chap. 1; Andrew Hacker, ed., *The Corporation Takeover* (New York: Harper and Row, 1964), Introduction; Ronald Segal, *The Americans: A Conflict of Creed and Reality*

(New York: The Viking Press, 1969), Chap. 1; Charles Reich, *The Greening of America* (New York: Random House, 1970), p. 89; Robin Marris, "Is the Corporate Economy a Corporate State?" *American Economic Review*, 62 No. 2 (May 1972), 103-115; J. K. Galbraith, *The New Industrial State* (Boston: Houghton Mifflin Co., 1967), and *Economics and the Public Purpose* (Boston: Houghton Mifflin Co., 1973); Daniel Bell, *The Coming of Post-Industrial Society* (New York: Basic Books, 1973); and W. Lloyd Warner, *The Corporation in the Emergent American Society* (New York: Harper and Row, 1962).

2. Neil H. Jacoby, *Corporate Power and Social Responsibility* (New York: Macmillan, 1973), and *The Impact of Large Firms on the U.S. Economy*, eds., J. F. Weston and Stanley I. Ornstein (Lexington, Mass.: D. C. Heath and Company, 1973).

3. *Studies by the Staff,* Cabinet Committee on Price Stability (Washington: U.S. Government Printing Office, 1969), p. 45.

4. Betty Bock, *Statistical Games and the "200 Largest" Industries: 1954 and 1968* (New York: The Conference Board, 1970).

5. Weston and Ornstein, *The Impact of Large Firms on the U.S. Economy*, p. 5.

6. Jacoby, *Corporate Power and Social Responsibility*, p. 32.

7. J. Fred Weston, "Pricing Behavior of Large Firms," *Western Economic Journal*, 10 (March 1972), 14.

8. A. D. H. Kaplan, *Big Enterprise in a Competitive System* (Washington, D.C.: Brookings Institution, 1954), pp. 286-290.

9. Weston and Ornstein, *The Impact of Large Firms on the U.S. Economy*, Chaps. 3-6.

10. See Harold Demsetz, *The Market Concentration Doctrine* (Washington, D.C.: AEI-Hoover Policy Studies, August 1973), for an admirable summary of the evidence on these matters. See also his "Market Structure, Market Rivalry and Public Policy," *Journal of Law and Economics*, 16, No. 1 (April 1973).

11. Edwin M. Epstein, *The Corporation in American Politics* (Englewood Cliffs, New Jersey: Prentice-Hall, Inc., 1969), p. 303.

12. See Roger G. Noll, *Reforming Regulation* (Washington, D.C.: Brookings Institution, 1971).

13. Proposals to accomplish these purposes appear in Chaps. 8-11 of my *Corporate Power and Social Responsibility, op.cit.*

SEVEN

Concentrated Industries

and

Economic Performance

Michael Granfield

Assistant Professor of Business Economics,
Graduate School of Management, UCLA

Assistant professor of business economics, Graduate School of Management, UCLA; B.A., University of Illinois, 1965; Ph.D., Duke University, 1970. On leave to Subcommittee on Antitrust and Monopoly of the Committee on the Judiciary, United States Senate.

Publications: *An Econometric Model of Residential Location,* Ballinger Publishing Co., 1974; "Housing Element of the General Plan for Los Angeles," Division of Real Estate Research, GBA, Chapters III and IV, UCLA, June 1970; (With S. Conrad and M. Oehm) "Toward a Better Analysis of Social Programs," *Inquiry* (December 1973); "Residential Location: A Comparative Econometric Analysis of Buffalo & Milwaukee," to *Applied Economics,* forthcoming; "A Further Look at Concentration & Profits," *Southern Economic Journal,* forthcoming.

1.   ECONOMIC AND PUBLIC POLICY ISSUES

This paper examines concentrated industries and their pattern of performance—how this performance has been evaluated, some of its implications for economic as well as political behavior, and finally why this topic is of interest. Economists generally describe concentrated industries as those in which the four top firms in the industry account for 50 percent or more of value added or value of shipments. We will be discussing profit patterns as an index of performance in industries which are allegedly dominated by anywhere from four to eight firms and in which these firms may earn an above-normal rate of return.

For economists, to view an industry which earns an above-normal rate of return dominated by few firms is, in and of itself, not an interesting proposition. It does not tell us about why that in fact is the case or why we are concentrating on examining the rate of return of only the top four or eight firms. In point of fact, the emphasis on this approach comes as much from a desire of people to understand political power as well as economic behavior.

In the 1920s economists were not particularly concerned about industries dominated by few firms because they felt that either existent rivalry between them, or potential entry, and hence new rivalry, would prevent the existence of serious monopoly abuses. However, in the 1930s, Gardiner Means, who was puzzled by the pricing behavior of large industries, felt that concentrated industries were not pricing according to basic supply and demand considerations and were engaged in administered pricing. He concluded that if these large firms were not pricing according to supply and demand, they must possess some monopoly power. I will not comment at length on what is some very poor economic analysis, since monopolists also price with respect to supply and demand. Further studies, in part motivated by Means's concerns, showed a weak relationship between rates of return and concentration ratios in certain industries. Those industries which were dominated by between four and eight firms seemingly were earning a higher rate of return than those industries in which there was less concentration.

2. THE STRUCTURAL THEORY OF ANTITRUST

Studies of this type have been referred to as the structural approach to economic performance. The structure of an industry is supposed to imply conduct, since it is alleged that collusion is facilitated. Specifically, the firms that dominate the industry over a long period of time are said to learn each other's behavior patterns so well that they are able to set prices above a competitive level and keep them there as if they were getting together in "smoke-filled rooms." That, in essence, is the structural contention with respect to industries dominated by large firms: there is a large degree of tacit collusion which yields prices above a competitive level with all of the welfare losses such conduct implies.

Currently the structural approach seemingly has more disciples in the political or public policy arena, at least based on recent studies and the implications of these studies, than in the economics arena. For example, the Federal Trade Commission has long adopted a structural approach in its merger and conduct suits. Recently however, they were embarrassed when they filed a conspiracy complaint against the largest vertically integrated oil companies alleging all kinds of criminal misconduct with respect to antitrust laws. In support of these charges they cited an upcoming study of the Federal Trade Commission, not published at the time of the complaint, which would study concentration patterns (structural approach) in the petroleum industry and would provide further evidence of collusive monopolistic behavior in the petroleum industry. However, when the study was released, it concluded that there was no evidence in the pattern of concentration in the petroleum industry to indicate it was any less competitive than the biscuit industry.[1] The Federal Trade Commission is now beginning a rather delicate back-stepping, by stating that there are times in which

the structural approach is not valid and we must rely on a conduct
approach; specifically, "smoke-filled rooms."

The Department of Justice, beginning with the Philadelphia Bank
Merger case, has placed increased emphasis on the structural approach
to examine economic conduct and performance.[2] In 1969, the Neal
Commission, appointed by President Johnson, indicated that those
industries in which the top eight firms accounted for 70 percent or more
of sales should be investigated for possible deconcentration.[3] In 1973
and in 1974, in the Senate Subcommittee on Antitrust and Monopoly,
its chairman, Senator Hart, has proposed the Industrial Reorganization Act, which is imbued with a great degree of structural
tests.

The Proposed Hart Bill

Provision I of the Hart Bill states: "The United States of America is
committed to a private enterprise system in a free market economy, and
the belief that competition spurs innovation, promotes productivity,
and preserves a democratic society, provides an opportunity for more
equitable distribution of wealth while avoiding the undue concentration of economic, social and political power." Note that Senator Hart is
not only concerned with the concentration of economic power, but also
with what it may imply for the concentration of political power.

Provision II states: "The decline of competition in industries with
oligopoly or monopoly power has contributed to unemployment, inflation, inefficiency and underutilization of economic capacity, and the
decline of exports; thereby rendering monetary and fiscal policies
inadequate and necessitating government market controls, subverting
our basic commitment to a free market economy." This harks back to
Means, who felt the depression should be blamed on the pricing behavior of large firms.

Provision III states: "The preservation of a private enterprise system, a free market economy, and a democratic society in the United
States of America requires legislation to supplement the policy of
antitrust laws through new enforcement mechanisms designed to re-
sponsively restructure industries dominated by oligopoly or monopoly
power." [4]

Senator Hart's tests for this monopoly power, and really his tests for monopoly political power, are any industry which: (1) in five of the last seven years leading firms have earned a higher than 15 percent rate of return on net worth after taxes; (2) there is no perceived price competition in the industry; and (3) the top four firms account for 50 percent or more or sales. Industries that meet any one of these criteria are definite candidates for deconcentration.

Furthermore, Senator Hart wishes to make our antitrust suits criminal rather than conduct suits. In other words, if an industry is found guilty under the Hart Bill—for example, it has a concentration above 50 percent—the burden of proof then rests upon the industry to prove it is not a monopolist. I, for one, do not understand how that proof could be established. How will price be measured? Will only list price be considered, or will other nonprice elements such as service be factored in? How many years must concentration prevail? What if only one firm earns a higher-than-15-percent rate of return?

The specific industries that Senator Hart has selected out for immediate attention are: chemicals and drugs, electrical machinery and equipment, electronic computing and communication equipment, energy, iron and steel, motor vehicles, and nonferrous metals.

3. THE CONCENTRATION HYPOTHESIS

The contention is that economic concentration tells us something about the conduct and performance of an industry. What is that hypothesis, or that argument or contention, really telling us? In essence, what the hypothesis states is that industries that have high concentration are more likely to collude because the concentration rato is a proxy for successful collusion. I find this a rather naïve view toward the whole problem of collusion. Specifically, when firms collude they face two challenges. One is to raise the price above the competitive level; the second is to restrict output such that firms seeing the higher price do not increase output, breaking down the agreement to raise price. In other words, if they cheat by increasing output, it puts a downward pressure on price and destroys the collusive agreement.

However, to date, most of the arguments about tacit collusion emphasize, following Gardiner Means, the price variable. But what is price? Price has many dimensions, as Professor Weston has pointed out in his article on pricing behavior of large corporations.[5] Price involves not only the price one pays at any given time but also its cyclical variation over the life cycle of the product. Most important in evaluating the actual price paid are such factors as distribution, service, quality control, warranty provisions, and so forth. All of these "nonprice" factors also must be agreed upon if a conspiracy price is not to fail. For example, every firm must agree on a twelve-month warranty or a fifteen-month warranty, quality of the product, and credit terms; and then, most critically, they must enforce the complex collusive agreement. Further, as demand grows in a market, each firm in the collusion must make sure that each member of the collusive agreement is not getting an inordinate share of new business. Therefore, some formula must be created to divide up new customers. Each of these agreements are enormous problems in terms of management and secrecy in that several thousand employees may typically be involved in the firms; the firms operate in numerable regional markets with numerable wholesalers, distributors, and retailers. All of these firms and levels must be accounted for and monitored if the collusive agreement is to be successful. This is not to say it cannot be done, or is not done. I only wish to point out that the cost of enforcing many collusive agreements could well exceed the benefits.[6] This cost factor not withstanding, let us turn now to the enforcement problem.

For a specific illustration of the problem of enforcement of tacit collusion, consider the complex problems of maintaining an overt conspiracy with actual meetings and written agreements. Specifically, consider the electrical equipment conspiracy of the late 1950s. My sources for this information are the court records as analyzed or paraphrased by the *Wall Street Journal, Fortune,* and *Business Week.*[7] This is a collusive agreement which had a high probability of success. The customers published, under legal obligation, what the sale price of the unit was an its technical specifications. Price-related information was available in the market, making detection of cheating very easy. All the sellers were known, and they were relatively few in number. Finally, many actual meetings between conspirators took place.

One of the explanations for entering into the collusive agreement that they offered was that, with decline in demand in the 1950s, it appeared that economies of scale in the industry would allow the large firms to drive the small firms out of business, making the large firms guilty of an antitrust violation for predatory price cutting. Clearly, another factor that drove them into a collusive agreement was the temptation for improved profits in this industry which were depressed for many of the firms. In order to insure a successful collusive agreement, not only did they fix prices, but they soon found that they had to bid for the business (e.g., for the TVA). Consequently, they decided to set up a numbering system to determine who would get the bid.

One of the basic findings coming out of the court testimony was the cheating conduct of the conspirators: they attended meetings only to find out what the low price would be so that they could undercut it.

Thus, even in this particular instance, where there was strong motivation and at least some large potential for success for a collusive agreement, there was a great deal of cheating and subsequent breakdown of the agreement. Further, the bureaucracy that they set up to monitor and effectuate the collusive agreement soon encompassed an enormous number of people, all of whom were potential leaks to the outside world. Ultimately the conspiracy broke down, leaks were determined, and the perpetrators prosecuted. Thus, obviously, it is tremendously difficult to make collusive agreements work. And this was not a passive agreement. They were getting together in "smoke-filled rooms." The Hart bill implies that the "smoke-filled room" effect can be accomplished through pricing as smoke signals in the market. But agreements on restricting outputs would also be required.

Given what appears to be a weak potential for a successful tacit collusive agreement, let us examine the empirical evidence for the collusion hypothesis.

4. DIRECT TESTS OF COLLUSION HYPOTHESIS: DEMSETZ

In its simplest state, the collusion hypothesis holds that firms in concentrated industries set price above a competitve level such that all firms in the industry are in part protected by the collusive price agreement. In unconcentrated industries no such agreement exists. Consequently, we would expect all firms in concentrated industries protected by a collusive umbrella to earn a higher rate of return than firms in unconcentrated industries. Professor Demsetz of UCLA has tested this hypothesis and found the evidence lacking. Specifically, he finds small firms in unconcentrated industries earn a higher rate of return than small firms in concentrated industries. Secondly, Demsetz finds that as concentration ratios increase, there is no evidence that the rate of return of small or large firms rises as a result of concentration itself. Further, he finds that large firms in concentrated industries earn a higher rate of return than smaller firms.[8] This implies that what is explaining the high rate of return in concentrated industries is their superior economic performance rather than any collusive agreement. Consequently, any policy to deconcentrate would result in higher production in higher cost, smaller firms; and higher prices for us all and the welfare loss that that implies. I think this is a very telling test of the direct implications of the collusive hypothesis. The direct implications of this hypothesis imply that small firms in concentrated industries earn a higher return than their counterparts in unconcentrated industries and would be positively correlated with concentration ratios, which they are not.

But rather than rely on this direct evidence, let us go back to some of the original studies that led to this hypothesis and try to understand why it had such great influence on public policy.

5. EARLIER TESTS OF THE CONCENTRATION HYPOTHESIS

As stated previously, Gardiner Means felt he had detected monopoly power in concentrated industries because they administered prices rather than letting the market determine them. He felt this aggravated the duration and extent of the depression since prices did not fall as much as demand decreases indicated. Means went beyond the administered-price thesis to determine that these same concentrated industries earned above-normal profits. Recent work by Weston and Lustgarten indicate that concentrated industries experienced lower rates of price increases than unconcentrated industries for most time segments since the end of World War II and especially during the recent inflationary periods.[9] Also, Stigler and Kindahl have indicated the faulty nature of Means's wholesale price data, which were list and not transaction prices.[10]

Nonetheless, based on the kinds of contentions proposed by Means,[11] a great number of empirical studies were launched to test the empirical relationship between concentration and profits. Most, although not all, found at least some positive correlation between concentration and profits.[12] This, however, is all they could claim to have found since they were not directly testing the implications of a collusive agreement on pricing and output decisions. Despite this obvious limitation, almost all the authors claimed that they had confirmed the existence of monopoly power for the industries they sampled. As a logical proposition, these interpretations appear dubious, since they did not either directly test the concentration-collusion hypothesis or its implications, as did Demsetz. Let us examine some other problems in interpreting the previous studies.

Professor Joe S. Bain found a positive correlation between concentration ratios and profits for the leading firms in 42 selected industries for the period 1936-40. However, he was not satisfied with this simple result since he felt that entry would erode collusive results. In other words, even if one had a successful tacit collusive agreement, other firms would be drawn in by the above-normal profits, and entry would ultimately undermine the collusive agreement. Therefore, Bain added to his analysis a consideration of barriers to entry as an independent explanatory factor in addition to concentration.[13]

The Bain barriers to entry were: (1) product differentiation—the advantage gained by a product already known by the consumer; (2) economies of scale—how much industry output must be accounted for before a small firm may enjoy the same cost advantage of a larger existing firm; and (3) capital entry barriers—how much capital must be raised to overcome these economies of scale and product differentiation disadvantages. He attempted to measure quantitatively these barriers to entry and then analyzed them together with concentration ratios. He concluded that industries which experienced both substantial barriers to entry and high concentration ratios would have higher profit rates.[14]

The Bain study was followed by a study by H. Michael Mann, who for the period of 1950-60 found essentially what Bain had found. Specifically, those industries with high barriers to entry and high concentration ratios were earning above-normal profits. He indicated in a qualified way that we ought to examine such industries for violation of our antitrust laws, and ultimately deconcentrate.[15]

An alternative approach directly testing the concentration hypothesis was an attempt to look at the difference between price and marginal cost. This study was done by Collins and Preston for food-manufacturing industries. The argument behind this study is to relate the differences between price and marginal cost as it relates to concentration. Their hypothesis is that the real test of monopoly power is the difference between price and marginal cost. Specifically, for competitive industries price equals marginal cost; hence, one test of the degree of monopoly power is to measure the difference between price and marginal cost, with monopoly power being correlated with the differential. They found the price-cost margin was correlated with concentration ratios and concluded that high concentration leads to successful tacit collusion.[16] However, a basic problem of price-cost margin studies is that their measured margin includes many elements of direct costs that bias their results.

6. PROBLEMS OF EARLIER STUDIES AND CORRECTIONS

Despite these results, all early studies suffered from serious deficiencies. One of the obvious problems with all of these studies is the simplicity of the relationship they hypothesize. Specifically, they correlate rates of return with concentration ratios indicating that, for them, the only thing that affects the profit rates of a firm is the structure of the industry. In technical terms, we call this specification bias. A second problem with these studies is sample size; more specifically, the size of the sample and its composition. For example, Bain relied only on the leading firms in an industry, which are most likely the top earners. A third statistical bias is produced by the time framework of the studies, e.g., the first Bain study covered four years, and the Mann study covered ten.

Recent studies have dealt with some of these obvious problems. Professor Ornstein built a much more sophisticated model to explain firm performance. Rather than looking at accounting profits, which produces innumerable difficulties due to the arbitrary nature of accounting techniques, he produced a superior measure, specifically, profits or rate of return as indicated by stock market values. He related this profit measure to concentration ratios, economies of scale, industry and firm growth rates, regional markets, and capital barriers. What he determined by employing this approach to explaining rate of return was that the concentration ratio had no significant role to play. Rather, such variables as economies of scale and firm growth rates explained firm performance, not concentration ratios.[17]

Furthermore, Ornstein studied the Collins and Preston work on price-cost margins. Here he found that their equation specification was wrong. Ornstein concluded:

The results demonstrate how well-intended authors such as Collins and Preston, are lead to fallacious results and conclusions by not presenting a rigorous theoretical basis for empirical tests. The area of industrial organization concerned with market structure and performance is largely empirically based, without a solid theoretical foundation. This comment points to a large theoretical gap requiring much future work.[18]

I think that is really the crux of the matter. Previous researchers have jumped into the empirical mass of data, found correlations, and then searched for a hypothesis to confirm their correlations. What we have to do if we are going to be good scientists is to start out with a rigorously deduced hypothesis, state what the implications of that hypothesis are, and then test it to the best of our abilities.

An alternative approach to these early studies is that taken by Professor Yale Brozen of Chicago. This approach is based on the concept of long-run equilibrium and entry. Specifically, Brozen contended that even if one found that leading firms in concentrated industries are earning above-normal returns for short periods of time, this does not mean that such returns persist over time. Perhaps we are simply sampling a period which in technical economic terms we call disequilibrium, and this high rate of return will attract entry and drive returns down to a normal level. What Brozen found was exactly that. In updating the Bain study of the years 1936-40 for 1953-57 and 1962-66, he found no persistence of high rates of return. Further, he found that these same industries were moving toward what approximates normal rates of return, whereas the unconcentrated industries in the 1936-40 time period, which were earning a below-normal return, had risen toward the norm. Therefore, Brozen determined that the Bain study was sampling industries and/or firms in disequilibrium. Brozen then expanded the original Bain study to include more industries and found no correlation between concentration and profits.[19]

When Brozen published his results, economists on the Neal Commission on Antitrust criticized Brozen's work and argued that he had arrived at his results by looking at the wrong industries. They then gave him a selection of industries to examine. When he examined these industries, he found no evidence of above-normal rates of return for any time period he examined.[20]

I also did some empirical work in this area. I took the Bain and Mann work and added the next ranking firm in the industry in order to test the sensitivity of the concentration-and-profits relationship. The next ranking firm in the industry is by any standard still a very large firm with large assets. I did not change the sample basis, and I kept the same industries and firms which Bain examined. In addition. I extended the time period in the Mann study to 1961-69.

My studies showed that in the period 1950-60 the Bain hypothesis, even with the extended sample, remained confirmed. Specifically, there is some positive correlation between concentration and profits for the industries selected. But this was not true for the 1961-69 period, nor was it true for the 1950-69 period. This indicates that the results that Bain found based on a very naïve and simple relationship is itself specific to the time period examined and to the sample which he chose to analyze. Data relating to mergers and acquisitions of these firms show that firms basically merge in areas where they have some managerial expertise. This is also supportive of the Demsetz contention that we are really analyzing the superior performance of large firms with respect to profits.[21]

Paul McCracken, former head of the Council of Economic Advisors, also testified before the Hart Committee, on evidence from a Federal Trade Commission study which had examined profit patterns of 112 selected industries. He compared the results for the concentration hypothesis when only the leading firm was included and when the second firm was also included. By including only the next ranking firm in the industry, the concentration hypothesis was not confirmed.[22] Professor Weston has examined 144 industries from the Compustat tapes on a year-by-year basis and, again using a simple correlation relationship, found no evidence for the concentration hypothesis.[23]

So in summary, it appears that recent findings based on a more sophisticated, economic approach incorporating a direct test of the collusion hypothesis, the notion of statistical refinements, and the concept of equilibrium find no evidence for the collusion hypothesis.

One other aspect of these studies, because it also bears on the political ramifications of studying the problem, is trends in concentration. Both Professors Adelman and Ornstein studied trends in concentration, and in general what they show is the following: Adelman tells us that from 1901 to 1947 there was some decline in overall industrial concentration for manufacturing firms. From 1947 to 1958 there has been virtually no change in concentration or amount of assets held by the leading manufacturing firms.[24] Ornstein updates the study through 1970 and in essence finds the same thing.[25]

Therefore, the hypothesis that the economy is becoming more concentrated over time with fewer and fewer firms controlling more aggregate assets is simply not true if we examine manufacturing firms as opposed to banks and other institutions.

Consequently, how do we explain, based on this recent evidence, the continuing popularity—and in Washington the increasing popularity —of the structural approach, and the increasing hostility with which large firms are met by public policy institutions in Washington?

7. ALTERNATIVE EXPLANATIONS OF THE POPULARITY OF THE CONCENTRATION HYPOTHESIS

Economic Explanation

To me, the answer does not lie in the area of economics; however, I will briefly state several reasons why it may. There is a tremendous misunderstanding concerning the monopoly versus the competitive model. The competitive model states that when there are atomistic firms, very small firms which have no discretionary power over price, we get very nice, welfare-pleasing results, since price equals marginal cost. When we have a one-firm monopoly, price exceeds marginal costs; there are losses, at least in a certain sense due to allocational inefficiency, and thus we get welfare losses because society is paying too high a price for the goods it consumes. However, there is no economic theory totally accepted by the profession that tells what happens in the intermediate stage. There is no economic theory that says we are better off when we go from six firms to seven firms, or six firms to twelve firms, or in point of fact from six firms to a hundred firms. Yet this has been the basis of almost all the merger settlements by the Federal Trade Commission and the Justice Department: that six firms is superior to five firms, which is superior to a four- or three-firm industry. However, we have no economic, empirical, or theoretical evidence to indicate that that in fact is the case. But this naïve view of competition is easy to comprehend, and, faced with the possibility of using the ambiguous theory of intermediate industry structures, the concentration hypothesis is preferred by advocates of atomism.

A second reason for persistence may be the concept of barriers to entry together with countervailing government power. Specifically, if there are real barriers to entry, you and I are not allowed to compete on equal grounds with existing firms. Something ought to be done to allow firms to, e.g., build automobiles on an equal par with General Motors. But before advancing public policy remedies, let us first look at the evidence with respect to barriers to entry.

First let us begin by examining economies of scale. Economies of scale implies some minimum percentage of industry output before an entrant can achieve the cost levels of the dominant firms in the industry. For example, an entrant must come into the automobile industry already producing, according to popular estimates, somewhere between 5 and 10 percent of industry output on day one. However, recent work by both John McGee and Fred Scherer indicates there is nothing fixed about the concept of technical economies of scale, since there are many ways to overcome pure production economies. Scherer indicates that in almost every industry he has examined in depth, small firms have always found ways to innovate around the problems of large-scale production economies. To illustrate, they adjust through better distribution systems, better product market systems, etc. Consequently, he finds no evidence that there have been true barriers to entry, although he paradoxically continues to stress that economies of scale do warrant the kind of attention received in traditional studies.[26]

Similarly, McGee finds the idea of estimating economies of scale an extremely complex one because it always deals with linear output and price decisions, whereas the real situation is indeed much more complex. For example, to understand cost structures we must deal with both the rate and planned volume at which the output is being produced. Given this multidimensional problem, he finds no evidence that one can successfully determine unequivocally, planned economies of scale. In addition, most analyses do not deal with the interaction between planned economies of scale of production, distribtion economies, advertising economies, and so forth. In short, the exact role of simple plant economies of scale is at best uncertain.[27]

A second alleged barrier is capital requirements. For this barrier to exist, capital markets must be imperfect: that is, only some firms are able to raise, at a competitive rate of interest, large amounts of capital to enter certain industries. The common view of this barrier is that it affects small firms trying to enter an industry. However, to be valid, it must also imply that large existing firms seeing attractive profits in some industry are also prevented from entering that industry. This seems to be an unlikely event because it precludes not only the entry of small firms but also the entry of large firms.[28] Further Professor Ornstein, in his study of concentration and profits, tested the capital entry barrier and found no evidence that it was a significant barrier to entry.[29] An alternative explanation to the entry-barrier contention is that there are not above-normal profits being earned.

The last commonly mentioned barrier is product differentiation. Differentiation is difficult to measure, so the usual proxy is the ratio of advertising to sales. However, recent studies indicate that advertising facilitates rather than bars entry.[30] Therefore, none of the alleged barriers to entry appears to be either clearly established or empirically verified.

Political Explanation

Given that the continued popularity of the structural approach cannot be explained on economic grounds, let me return to the theme I expressed originally: the political ramifications of the issue. Public policy is not interested in economic power for economic reasons but is interested in economic power because it allegedly leads directly to political power. The curtailment of abusive political power is sought, and of course Watergate has fueled the flame of this particular aim. (However, there is also strong evidence of the power of government to levy tribute on business firms and other ogranizations.) I think that Senator Hart has expressed this concern quite well:

Legislation for inflation should also include some action against the various conglomerations of power that are impeding the effective operation of the government, and indeed our society. The problem however remains that we need some ways of dealing with it. Action cannot be postponed until all the studies are completed. . . . I agree on both points that we know far too little and that action cannot be postponed. And it can't be postponed for reasons that are both social and political. . . . Are there not some instances in which we must punish economic success for the sake of political democracy? [31]

A recent editorial in the *Washington Post* makes the same point. The *Post* is complaining about campaign abuses, and it states: "It appears that the pattern of campaign abuses comes from, most recently, the milk industry, the petroleum industry, and the airlines." They further state, "This seems to have something to do with government intervention in these industries." [32]

Firms or groups of individuals become interested in the government because the government is interested in them, or somehow is intimately involved in their affairs. However, I think it is an oversimplification to think that large firms dominate this process. There is no question that economic power implies or will yield some degree of political power; but I think the question of gains from political power is much more complex than looking at simple concentration ratios and implying that they are also concentration ratios of political power.

Petroleum Industry Concessions

To illustrate, take the petroleum industry. Consider the various concessions it has received over time and what has led to these concessions.

Let us first look at the oil import program, the mandatory oil import program of 1959. This program does not really favor the large firms who operate relatively large refineries and are building new capacities, or at least have the capacity to build new, large refineries. Because of the way it was structured and the way exemptions were granted under the oil import program, it favored smaller refineries over large refiners. Therefore, it was the coalition of large and small petroleum refiners that put the political muscle behind the oil import program.[33]

A second concession given the petroleum industry which has led to cartel results is the Texas Railroad Commission and prorationing. Prorationing is the device by which the Commission divides up among common property holders of oil reserves the amount each can take out of the ground. It also restricted total output from the state of Texas. Again, the way the program is set up tends to favor smaller wells, and politically the people on the Texas Railroad Commission have their stock interest in small explorer firms rather than the majors.[34] Numbers therefore appear to be at least as, if not more important than, absolute financial size.

The oil depletion allowance, based on my analysis, helps the large and small producer equally. However, in this instance it was not only the petroleum industry that lobbied for this concession, it was all explorative mineral industries. This does not mean the concession is satisfactory but rather that there was a wide political coalition of large and small firms from high- to low-concentration industries that argued for depletion allowances.

Finally, the Cost of Living Council and the Emergency Petroleum Allocation Act, which impose price controls on the petroleum industry, came into existence despite vigorous efforts on the part of all major manufacturing firms and others to restrict the nature and imposition of price controls.

J. B. Mitchell, who has written an energy primer for public policy in which he talks about our initial oil legislation which led to surpluses, and the more recent legislation which has led to shortages, states:

Significantly there is one group that always benefits from a shortage policy or a surplus policy. A rationing procedure must always be established to allocate the shortage among consumers or the surplus among producers. The power to influence these rationing decisions is of considerable value. Thus politicians, bureaucrats, Washington lawyers, and the communications media are the direct beneficiaries. As a practical matter the benefits occurring to this group may dominate the entire decision-making process.[35]

I think his point is well taken.

It appears that what bestows political power is some combination of financial resources and numbers, and how both of these are translated into votes.

8. ANALYSIS OF POLITICAL INFLUENCE: "MONOPOLY, INC."

I will end with a simplified view of the nature of political influence and how it is purchased. Clearly, the people who bestow political influence are politicians. If we assume that politicians have reelection as their major goal, they must somehow influence and obtain votes. Hence, to influence politicians one can use cash or direct promises of votes. Clearly, cash is less desired than the votes themselves. Consequently, if you can come to a politician and promise him X number of votes, you are much more influential than if you can bring him X amount of cash. He can obviously use the cash to influence and attempt to purchase votes through the use of the media and other information devices. However, he clearly prefers the certainty of X votes.

For example, from my short experience on the Hill, the impact of letters to senators, and even more particularly to congressmen, is enormous. It is interesting to see how positions, particularly in the House, begin to turn as the mail begins to turn. For most staffs, about half of their time is spent simply monitoring and answering the mail. Therefore legislators, particularly congressmen, are sharply attuned to what their letters are saying because that is their most efficient way of finding out what constituents want, and that becomes what politicians want, because they want reelection.

In order to obtain votes or cash, politicians must offer something. In a sense, they must sell something. Assume politicians, or as a collective unit the government, sells from a store entitled "Monopoly, Incorporated" or the "Cartel Club." This particular store sells outright monopoly or partial monopolies. An outright monopoly would be similar to the Yellow Taxi Cab Company franchises in many cities, or a utility of some sort (whether there are economic grounds behind it or not). Alternatively, the government can license, or give you the power to license, your profession. Or they can pass a law that says, for example, that professional sports are immune from antitrust violations, which enables the owners to impose a reserve clause on their participants. Further, the store can sell a partial monopoly, such as an import quota or a tariff. Finally, if you are quite imaginative or think you have a comparative advantage in enforcement, they will offer you price fixing; witness the Civil Aeronautics Board, the Interstate Commerce Commission, fair trade laws, prorationing experience, etc.

Possibly more interesting than the sale of monopoly and concessions is the question of where the inventory comes from. Where do they get these monopolies to sell? Paradoxically, some come indirectly from the "Nader Co-op." Specifically, "Monopoly, Inc." must wait for consumer groups and other activists to become involved with an issue; to become so involved that they necessitate that either the government take over the industry (which is unusual in this country although the pressure is growing) or, more realistically, that the government regulate and control the industry so that consumers' interests are promoted. This regulatory legislation puts the goods on the store shelf. Once they are on the shelf, we as "consumers" have a chance to bid for them. There is no reason to think that an ICC or a CAB will not serve our interests. But as it turns out the politician sells the goods, as any good store owner will, to that group which offers the highest price: that group which stands to benefit (net) greatest from the concession and which is most efficient in organizing its interests. Consequently, it is not surprising that monopolies are always sold to that person(s) who markets rather than buys the goods. This is *totally* predictable. We have given government property rights over a particular allocation of resources. It is thus not surprising that politicians and/or regulators will sell to the highest bidder. This does not mean it necessarily involves bribery or any illegal activities; it simply may involved a legal contribution or promise of votes.

Consequently, if Senator Hart is interested in the demise of political power, what he should be most interested in is the demise of the "Monopoly, Incorporated" store. One way to accomplish this would be simply to have government at the federal, state, and local levels be prevented from granting a property right which is inconsistent and contradicts current antitrust statutes. Certainly, granting a group of firms the right to fix prices seems to be in opposition to antitrust statutes.

In order to provide some proof of this monopoly allegation and its attendant analogies, look at industries employing Gardiner Means's type test; namely, where prices are rising fastest. Specifically, in the last ten years prices have risen faster in the medical industry, followed closely by the construction industry and maritime interests, than in any other sectors of the country. It is not too surprising that doctors have a substantial degree of monopoly power. The source of that monopoly is in essence barriers to entry and work-rulers restrictions. We find a similar case with construction unions. Further, we find that there has been a large campaign recently in Washington to prevent legislation being passed which would enable druggists to advertise the price of drugs. This is further evidence of an unconcentrated group that has a concentrated interest, and votes as a block to achieve its goal at the "Monopoly, Incorporated" store—the government.

In summary, the buying and selling of political influence is directly related to the size and value of the inventory in the "Monopoly, Inc." store. Therefore, if we wish to curb the extent of such alleged corruption, we must realize that regulation can never be the optimal solution to problems of public policy. We must constantly seek to employ the power of the "invisible hand" to reduce the inventory of the "Monopoly, Inc." store.

NOTES

1. Douglas Webbink and Joseph Mulholland, *Concentration Levels and Trends in the Energy Sector of the U.S. Economy*, FTC Staff Report (January 1974).
2. United States v. Philadelphia National Bank, 374 U.S. 321 (1963).
3. Bureau of National Affairs, *Antitrust Trade Regulation Report*, No. 411 (May 1969).
4. S. 3832, 92nd Congress, 2nd Session; reintroduced as S. 1167 in 93rd Congress.
5. J. Fred Weston, "Pricing Behavior of Large Firms" *Western Economic Journal* (March 1972), pp. 1-18.
6. Frederick M. Scherer, *Industrial Market Structure and Economic Performance* (Chicago: Rand McNally & Co., 1970), pp. 146-148.
7. "Collusion Among Electrical Equipment Manufacturers," *Wall Street Journal*, January 10, 1967.
8. Harold Demsetz, "Industry Structure, Market Rivalry, and Public Policy," *Journal of Law and Economics* (April 1973), pp. 1-9.
9. J. Fred Weston and Steven H. Lustgarten, "Concentration and Inflation," in Columbia Law School Conference on *Industrial Concentration: The Economic Issues* (March 1974).
10. George J. Stigler and James K. Kindahl, *The Behavior of Industrial Prices*, National Bureau of Economic Research (New York: Columbia University Press, 1970).
11. Senate Document 13 (January 17, 1935), 74th Congress, 1st Session.
12. Leonard Weiss, "Quantitative Studies of Industrial Organization," in *Frontiers of Quantitative Economics*, ed., M. D. Intriligator (New York: North-Holland Co., 1971), pp. 184-225.
13. Joe S. Bain, "Relation of Profit Rate to Industry Concentration: American Manufacturing, 1936-1940," *Quarterly Journal of Economics* (August 1951), pp. 293-324.
14. *Ibid.*, p. 323.
15. H. Michael Mann, "Seller Concentration, Barriers to Entry, and Rates of Return in Thirty Industries, 1950-60," *Review of Economics and Statistics* (August 1966), pp. 296-307.
16. Norman R. Collins and Lee E. Preston, "Concentration and Price-Cost Margins in Food Manufacturing Industries," *Journal of Industrial Economics* (July 1966), pp. 226-242.
17. Stanley I. Ornstein, "Concentration and Profits," *Journal of Business* (October 1972), pp. 519-541.

18. Stanley I. Ornstein, "Empirical Uses of Price-Cost Margins," Working Paper No. 37, Business Competion and Public Policy Center, UCLA, Graduate School of Management.

19. Yale Brozen, "The Antitrust Task Force Deconcentration Recommendation," *Journal of Law and Economics* (October 1970), pp. 229-292.

20. Yale Brozen, "The Persistence of 'High Rates of Return' in High-Stable Concentration Industries," *Journal of Law and Economics* (October 1971), pp. 501-512.

21. Michael E. Granfield, "A Further Look at Concentration and Profits," Working Paper No. 39, Business Competition and Public Policy Center, UCLA Graduate School of Management.

22. U.S. Senate Hearings before Subcommittee on Antitrust and Monopoly, March 29, 1973.

23. J. Fred Weston, "Performance in Concentrated Industries," presentation in *Hearings before the Subcommittee on Antitrust and Monopoly of the Committee on the Judiciary United States Senate,* 93rd Congress, 1st Session on S. 1167, Part I: General Views, p. 225.

24. Morris A. Adelman, "Changes in Industrial Concentration," in *Monopoly Power and Economic Performance,* ed., E. Mansfield (New York: W. W. Norton & Co., Inc., 1968), pp. 78-83.

25. Stanley I. Ornstein, "Trends and Changes in Concentration in U.S. Manufacturing Industry: 1947-70," Working Ppaer No. 35, Business Competition and Public Policy Center, UCLA, Graduate School of Management.

26. Frederick M. Scherer, "Economics of Scale and Industrial Concentration," in *Industrial Concentration: The Economic Issues, loc. cit.,* pp. 1-70.

27. John S. McGee, "Efflciency and Economies of Size," in *Industrial Concentration: The Economic Issues, loc. cit.,* pp. 71-130.

28. In point of fact, no one, including Joe Bain, has alleged that this is the most significant barrier. This discussion casts doubt on the actual existence of such a barrier, critical or not.

29. Stanley I. Ornstein, "Concentration and Profits," *op.cit.*

30. Yale Brozen, "Entry Barriers: Advertising and Product Differentiation," in *Industrial Concentration: The Economic Issues, loc. cit.,* pp. 135-165.

31. Senate hearings on S. 1167, March, 1973.

32. *Washington Post,* March 27, 1974.

33. J. D. Mitchell, *An Energy Primer* American Enterprise Institute, Washington, D.C. (March 1974).

34. *Ibid.,* p. 27.

35. *Ibid.,* p. 40.

EIGHT

Economists and Public Policy

R. H. Coase

Professor of Economics
University of Chicago Law School

Editor, Journal of Law and Economics; B. Com., London School of Economics, 1932; D.Sc., University of London, 1951. Fields: 7abd, lab. Publications: British Broadcasting, *A Study in Monopoly,* 1950; "The Nature of the Firm," *Economica,* 1937; "The Problem of Social Cost," *Journal of Law and Economics,* 1960. Research: The Political Economy of Radio and Television; Historical Studies of British Public Utilities.

Assistant lecturer, lecturer, reader, London School of Economics, 1935-51; professor of economics, University of Buffalo, 1951-58; professor of economics, University of Virginia, 1958-64; professor of economics, University of Chicago, since 1964. He has been editor of *The Journal of Law and Economics* since 1964.

The aspect of large enterprise that I will be examining in this chapter is the study of economics, and the performance that I will be appraising is not that of corporations but of my colleagues in the economics profession. The particular aspect of their work that I will be examining will be the part that economists play in the determination of public policy.

CAN ECONOMICS CONTRIBUTE TO PUBLIC POLICY ISSUES?

I know, of course, that there are some economists who argue that economics is a positive science and that all we can do is to explain the consequences that follow from various economic policies. We cannot say whether one policy is preferable to another, because to do so would require us to introduce value judgments, in the making of which we have no special competence. Thus we can say that certain agricultural policies (say collectivization) will lead to widespread starvation, but we cannot say whether collectivization is or is not desirable. Such self-restraint is I think unnecessary. We share (at least in the West) a very similar set of values, and there is little reason to suppose that the value judgments of economists are particularly eccentric. There will, of course, be instances in which, knowing the consequences of a change in policy, there will be differences in opinion as to whether the change is desirable. But such cases are, I believe, exceptions, and can be treated as such. I agree with Milton Friedman's judgment that "currently in the Western World, and especially in the United States, differences about economic policy among disinterested citizens derive predominantly from different predictions about the economic consequences of taking action—differences that in principle can be eliminated by the progress of positive economics—rather than from fundamental differences in basic values, differences about which men can ultimately only fight." [1] Of course, if this is so, it has the result that an analysis of the consequences of alternative social arrangements becomes a prescription for policy (since we all share the same values). Thus it hardly matters, once it is established that a certain policy will lead to widespread starvation, whether we add that the policy would be undesirable—although to refrain from doing so on principle seems like an affectation. In general, one would expect that a statement of the consequences of alternative policies would bring its policy recommendations with it.

Whether they should or not, few economists do in fact refrain from making pronouncements on public policy: although the state of the economy (both here and elsewhere) suggests either that the advice given is bad or if good, that it is ignored. Of course, there is the other possibility, more disturbing from some points of view but reassuring from others, that the advice is disregarded, whether it is good or bad. I happen to think that we are appallingly ignorant about many aspects of the working of the economic system, at least so far as that part of economics is concerned in which I am particularly interested—the economics of the firm and industry. I think we know very little about the forces which determine the organization of industry or the arrangements which firms make in their transactions with one another. We have, of course, been told that when we consider the economics of the system as a whole, what is termed macroeconomic policy, that things are very different, at least since the appearance of Keynes' *General Theory*, and that we now know how to secure full employment coupled with a stable price level. I leave to others more knowledgeable in this field whether our present troubles are due to ignorance, impotence in affecting policy, or some other cause. But I do seem to have detected in recent years a degree of humility among workers in this field not hitherto observed.

Yet having said this, I would not wish to argue that economists do not have something valuable to contribute to the discussion of public policy issues. The problem is that economists seem willing to give advice or questions about which we know very little and on which our judgments are likely to be fallible while what we have to say which is important and true is quite simple—so simple indeed that little or no economics is required to understand it. What is discouraging is that it is these simple truths which are so commonly ignored in the discussion of economic policy.

THE ROLE OF PRICE IN ALLEVIATING SHORTAGES

It requires no great economics to know that at a lower price, consumers will buy a greater quantity. Or to know that as price falls, producers will be willing to supply less. Even the combining of these two notions to show that, if the price is put low enough, producers will not be willing to supply as much as consumers wish to buy (so that what is called a "shortage" will result) is easy enough to understand. Indeed, the essentials of such a situation would be understood by many who have not studied economics at all. Yet consider an example. In the early 1960s, the Federal Power Commission began to regulate the field price of natural gas. The price was frozen at the 1959-60 level. It became apparent that this was lower than the price would have been without regulation. What followed was what one would expect. Consumption was encouraged; the discovery and exploitation of natural gas was discouraged. The effect of the regulation was at first masked by the short-term fall in the cost of coal and by a reduction in the quality of what was supplied (the consumer had less assurance of the availability of the gas in future). But as time went on, the nature of the regulation-induced shortage of natural gas (to use Professor MacAvoy's phrase) became obvious to the meanest intelligence, and the Federal Power Commission began to take steps to raise the price.

A number of studies have been made (by Professor Paul MacAvoy and others) and there is general agreement about what happened. One of these studies was carried out by Professor Edmund Kitch at the University of Chicago Law School and was published in the *Journal of Law and Economics* in 1968.[2] Later Professor Kitch decided that it would be a good idea if he updated his study. He then presented his findings in Washington, D.C., in 1971 in a talk entitled "The Shortage of Natural Gas."[3] A large part of the audience consisted of Washington journalists, members of the staff of congressional committees concerned with energy problems, and others with similar jobs. They displayed little interest in the findings but a great deal in discovering who had financed the study. Many seem to have been convinced that the law-economics program at the University of Chicago had been "bought" by the gas industry. In fact, this study had not been financed by funds provided by any organization of any kind connected with the gas or oil industries. But a large part of the audience seemed to live in a simple world in which anyone who thought prices should rise was pro-industry and anyone who wanted prices to be reduced was pro-consumer. I could have explained that the essentials of Professor Kitch's argument had been put forward earlier by Adam Smith—but most of the audience would have assumed that he was someone else in the pay of the American Gas Association.

Adam Smith does not, of course, mention the natural gas industry, which did not exist in his time, but he deals with what is the same problem in his discussion of the corn trade. By corn, Adam Smith means, of course, wheat. I quote Adam Smith: "The interest of the inland [corn] dealer, and that of the great body of the people, how opposite soever they may at first sight appear, are, even in the years of the greatest scarcity, exactly the same. It is his interest to raise the price of his corn as high as the real scarcity of the season requires, and it can never be his interest to raise it higher. By raising the price he discourages the consumption, and puts everybody more or less, but particularly the inferior ranks of people, upon thrift and good management. . . . If by not raising the price high enough he discourages the consumption so little, that the supply of the season is likely to fall short of the consumption of the season, he not only loses a part of the profit which he might otherwise have made, but he exposes the people to suffer before the end of the season, instead of the hardships of a dearth, the dreadful horrors of a famine." [4] But, as Smith points out, since the dealer will maximize his profits by adjusting the price at which he sells so that consumption over the season is equal to the supply he is not likely to do this. Adam Smith adds: "Whoever examines, with attention, the history of the dearths and famines which have afflicted any part of Europe, during either the course of the present or that of the two preceding centuries, of several of which we have pretty exact accounts, will find, I believe, that a dearth never has arisen from any combination among the inland dealers in corn, nor from any other cause but a real scarcity, occasioned sometimes, perhaps, and in some particular place, by the waste of war, but in by far the greatest number of cases, by the fault of the seasons; and that a famine has never arisen from any other cause but the violence of government attempting, by improper means, to remedy the inconvenience of a dearth. . . . When the government, in order to remedy the inconveniences of a dearth, orders all the dealers to sell their corn at what it supposes a reasonable price, it either hinders them from bringing it to market, which may sometimes produce a famine even in the beginning of the season; or if they bring it thither, it enables the people, and thereby encourages them to consume it so fast, as must necessarily produce a famine before the end of the season. The unlimited, unrestrained freedom of the corn trade, as it is the only effectual preventative of the miseries of a famine, so it is the best palliative of the inconveniences of a dearth; for the inconveniences of a real scarcity cannot be remedied; they can only be palliated." [5] Of course, the beneficial role of the merchant in palliating the inconvenience of the scarcity is not understood. "In years of scarcity the inferior ranks of people impute their distress to the avarice of the corn merchant, who becomes the object of their hatred and indignation." [6] And he points out that this hostility to the merchant shows itself in the laws against "engrossing and forestalling," that is, the buying and holding of an inventory to sell at a higher price. Of course, Adam Smith is able to show that the merchant will find his holding of stocks profitable only when it is desirable that he should do so. And he comments: "The popular fear of engrossing and forestalling may be compared to the popular terrors and suspicions of witchcraft." [7] Adam Smith here attempts to discredit the idea that businessmen by holding stocks make prices higher than they would otherwise be by likening it to a belief in witchcraft. Such an analogy would be less effective today—we also believe in witchcraft.

PRICE CONTROLS IN HISTORICAL PERSPECTIVE

In the two hundred years which have passed since Adam Smith wrote, many economists have argued along much the same lines about the futility of a policy of holding prices below the competitive level. One of these was Edwin Cannan, of the London School of Economics, who wrote about sixty years ago. He was, of course, speaking of the price controls established in Britain at the beginning of World War I. He describes the public response to a rise in price: "Buyers who have to pay higher prices suddenly become either 'the poor' forced to reduce their consumption of necessary articles or else employers of a particularly needy and deserving class which will be thrown out of work by the rise. All the injured persons are at once represented as being iniquitously robbed by an unscrupulous gang of speculators, middlemen, blood-sucking capitalists, or rack-renting landlords against whom all the resources of the State ought to be brought forthwith. The ideal somewhat vaguely held seems to be an immediate return to the prices of a few months or a year ago." [8] Of course, Cannan argues against price controls in the usual way. But he points to a paradoxical aspect of the situation: "When the price of a thing goes up, [people] abuse, not the buyers nor the persons who might produce it and do not do so, but the persons who are producing and selling it, and thereby keeping down its price." [9] So, if there is a "shortage" of wheat or beef, or oil, we abuse those who are producing all the wheat, beef, or oil that we have and without whose efforts the "shortage" would have been still greater. The reason why people show this hostility is that, as Cannan points out, if there is an unusual rise in prices, people "are perfectly convinced that the rise with which they have to contend for the moment is unnatural, artificial, and wholly unjustifiable, being merely the wicked work of people who want to enrich themselves, and who are given the power to do so not by the economic conditions . . . but apparently by some absolutely direct and inexplicable interference of the Devil. This has been so since the dawn of history . . . but no amount of historical retrospect seems to be of much use. The same absurdity crops up generation after generation." [10]

WHY ARE BASIC ECONOMIC TRUTHS NOT ACCEPTED?

I began this paper by saying that economists in their discussion of public policy often deal with questions which are difficult to analyze, about which we know very little, and on which, therefore, our recommendations, if followed, would very likely make things worse. On the other hand, the advice we do have to offer which would be valuable, if followed, consists of a few simple truths. However, history indicates that these are simple truths which people find it easy to reject—or ignore. When I first began thinking about what I would say, I did not anticipate the present oil problem (and I was not alone). But the character of the public discussion of this problem suggests that we are no better than those who went before us. We are a generation whose time has come. We observe the same attitudes that Cannan described—"the rise [of price] with which we have to contend at the moment" being "unnatural, artificial, and wholly unjustifiable . . . the wicked work of people who want to enrich themselves." This raises the question of what the role of an economist should be in a world which rejects the only solidly based advice that he has to give.

Frank Knight, in his presidential address to the American Economic Association in 1950, posed this question—and gave an appropriately depressing answer. "I have been increasingly moved to wonder whether my job is a job or a racket, whether economists, and particularly economic theorists, may not be in a position that Cicero, citing Cato, ascribed to the augurs of Rome—that they should cover their faces or burst into laughter when they met on the street. . . . The free-traders, as has been said, win the debates but the protectionists win the elections; and it makes little difference in our policy which party wins, the avowed protectionists or the professed free-traders. Inflation is of course to be brought on as a more pleasant alternative to taxation and then suppressed by law and police action. . . . The serious fact is that the bulk of the really important things that economics has to teach are things that people would see for themselves if they were willing to see. And it is hard to believe in the utility of trying to teach what men refuse to learn or even seriously listen to. . . . Can there be any use in explaining, if it is needful to explain, that fixing a price below the free-market level will create a shortage and one above it a surplus? But the public's oh's and ah's and yips and yaps at the shortage of residential housing and surpluses of eggs and potatoes as if these things presented problems——any more than getting one's footgear soiled by deliberately walking in the mud." [11] Knight said that, in consequence of this, his interest had tended to shift away from economic theory "to the question of why people so generally, and the learned elite in particular, as they express themselves in various ways choose nonsense instead of sense" [12]—which is one possible response to the situation, although not, I think, the only one open to us. Knight also says something else which is, I think, helpful to those of us who are looking for an alternative response: "Explanations of policy might conceivably get farther if we . . . ask *why* men believe and practice nonsense but in general act so much less irrationally than they argue—and what follows from that." [13]

If we took seriously the arguments used by those who advocate price controls and similar measures, we would expect much more extreme, and less sensible, proposals than are actually put forward. Thus, some senators believe that lower prices for gasoline would benefit consumers—so they introduce a measure in Congress which would make the gasoline prices of last December mandatory, not the still lower prices that prevailed in the 1930s. The Federal Power Commission undertook in 1961 to regulate the field price of natural gas—so the level of prices which it determined should be charged in future was that prevailing in 1959-60. As Cannan said, writing some sixty years ago and about a different country: "The ideal somewhat vaguely held seems to be a return to the prices of a few months or a year ago." Similarly, politicians may make speeches which favor the elimination of all pollution; their proposals are much more moderate. Furthermore, I seem to observe that as the harm inflicted by the policy increases, the strength of the support for that policy decreases—which leads, if not to the elimination of the policy, at any rate to a moderation of it. The Federal Power Commission finally did act to raise the field price of natural gas, although it no doubt acted more slowly and made a smaller change than most economists would have liked. With a rise in the price of oil, concern about the fate of the caribou in Alaska became less pressing, and the Alaska Pipe Line is now likely to be built. Although controls, such as price and wage controls, are introduced to prevent the basic economic forces from working, a study of the history of controls would show, I believe, that, over a longer period, there have been very few controls which have not been modified to take them into account, or even abandoned, so that market forces have free sway. My conclusion is that, although a policy may be misguided, we should not assume that its range, severity, and duration are not kept in check by recognition of the extent of the harm it produces. I do not myself understand why the political system operates in the way it does. Whether the interests opposed to the policy tend to become relatively stronger in the political arena as the amount of the harm inflicted by the policy increases, or whether recognition of the amount of harm plays a more direct role in the political process, or both of these factors operate, I do not know, although it would be my judgment that both of these factors exert some weight. At any rate, it may be that there is room for economists' views on public policy to play a valuable part in this process of modification and change, even though they will usually not be able to exercise a decisive influence over the choice of the policy itself. Certainly, however ill-advised policies may be, they are not in their administration devoid of sense. The demand for nonsense seems to be subject to the universal law of demand: we demand less of it when the price is higher.

THE POTENTIAL CONTRIBUTIONS OF ECONOMISTS

A more optimistic view of the role of the economist in the formulation of public policy or, at any rate, of his future role, was presented by Professor George Stigler in his presidential address to the American Economic Association in 1964, entitled, "The Economist and the State." [14] Professor Stigler argued that economists in the past have been willing to express views on the role of the state in economic affairs without making any serious study of how the state did in fact carry out the tasks entrusted to it or making any systematic investigation of the comparative performance of state and private enterprise. This was true both for those, like Smith and Marshall, who wanted to limit government intervention in the economic system and for those, like Jevons, Pigou, and a host of others, who were in favor of an expanding governmental role. Stigler's comments on our predecessors seem a little harsh—they faced difficulties which we do not encounter, they were few in number, and they were mainly engaged (particularly the better among them) in developing the analysis of a pricing system—but I do not wish particularly to quarrel with his main conclusion. I have argued that our knowledge is very limited—and we are able to read what our predecessors wrote.

Professor Stigler ascribes the lack of influence of economists on the formulation of public policy—which he asserts and I would not wish to deny—to their ignorance. "Lacking real expertise, and lacking also evangelical ardor, the economist has had little influence upon the evolution of economic policy." [15] But that is the past. The future, according to Professor Stigler, will be very different. "The age of quantification is now full upon us. We are armed with a bulging arsenal of techniques of quantitative analysis, and of a power—as compared to untrained common sense—comparable to the displacement of archers by cannon. . . . the desire to measure economic phenomena is not in the ascendent. . . . It is a scientific revolution of the very first magnitude. . . . I am convinced that economics is finally at the threshold of its golden age—nay, we already have one foot through the door. The revolution in our thinking has begun to reach public policy, and soon it will make irresistible demands upon us. It will become inconceivable that the margin requirements on securities markets will be altered once a year without knowing whether they have even a modest effect. It will become impossible for an import-quota system to evade the calculus of gains and costs. It will become an occasion for humorous nostalgia when arguments for private and public performance of a given economic activity are conducted by reference to the phrase, external economies, or by recourse to a theorem on perfect competition. . . . I assert, not that we should make the studies I wish for, but that no-one can delay their coming. . . . That we are good theorists is not open to dispute. . . . the last half century of economics certifies the immense increase in the power, the care, and the courage of our quantitative researches. Our expanding theoretical and empirical studies will inevitably and irresistibly enter into the subject of public policy, and we shall develop a body of knowledge essential to intelligent policy formulation. And then, quite frankly, I hope that we become the ornaments of democratic society whose opinions on economic policy shall prevail." [16]

I was present when Professor Stigler delivered his address and, as he ended with these words, it was hard to restrain a cheer. When the immediate impact of this eloquent and moving address had passed,

Stigler's assertions brought to mind Pope's couplet: "Hope springs eternal in the human breast;/Man never is, but always to be, blest."

But even though we do not believe that such a glittering prospect lies ahead of us, we need not despair. If, as I am inclined to believe, economists cannot usually affect the main course of economic policy, their views may make themselves felt in small ways. An economist who, by his efforts, is able to postpone by a week a government program which wastes a $100 million a year (what I would consider a modest success), has by his action earned his salary for the whole of his life. Indeed, if we compute the total annual salaries of all economists engaged in research on public policy issues (or questions related to this), which might amount to $20 million (or some similar figure), it is clear that this expenditure (or one much larger) would be justified if it led to a minuscule increase in the gross national product. It is not necessary to change the world to justify our salaries. But does the advice of economists on public policy issues improve the situation in those cases in which it does have some influence? I take Professor Stigler's main purpose to be, not to raise our morale, but to induce us to change our ways so that our advice will be worth following. If, as a result, we achieve my modest aim, we will at least earn our keep. If Professor Stigler's view of the future is correct, we will confer a great benefit on mankind—and be grossly underpaid.

The advice that we have had to offer in the past that was valuable —what I have called the simple truths—was, of course, the implications of a theoretical system which, while its range was restricted, has been confirmed time after time. The assumption of the theory is that producers want to make as much money as possible and that consumers want to get as much for their money as they can. Or, put more generally, and with more applications, it is assumed that people tend, in the main, to pursue their own self-interests. It has proved a very robust theory. But, of course, without knowledge of magnitudes (though they could sometimes be inferred), there were a lot of questions that the theory could not answer. But this hardly explains why the theory has been ignored for those questions for which it could give answers.

Professor Stigler pins his high hopes for the future on the growth in quantitative work. But this development is not without its costs. It absorbs resources which might otherwise be devoted to the development of our theory and to empirical studies of the economic system of a nonquantitative character. Aspects of the economic system which are difficult to measure tend to be neglected. It diverts attention from the economic system itself to the technical problems of measurement. I do not mean to suggest that we should avoid quantitative work. But it is well to remember that there is no such thing as a free statistic.

THE VALUE OF ECONOMIC ANALYSIS

I would like to illustrate my view that nonquantitative work, or at least work with only the crudest form of quantification, can be of value by means of an example. About 1960 Senator Kefauver was holding hearings into the drug industry and particularly into its practices in introducing new drugs. The main thrust of the hearings was to suggest that the prices paid were too high but even more that the drugs were often of little or even of dubious value. Senator Kefauver concluded that it would be desirable to regulate the introduction of new drugs. At the time this proposal was under consideration the tragic side effects of the use of thalidomide by pregnant women became known. The result was to generate so much support for drug regulation that the Kefauver proposal, which might otherwise have failed to secure congressional approval, was enacted into law in 1962. Was it wise to do this? Consider what one economist said early in 1965 and long before the effects of this new law could be known. "I ask myself a question: Suppose I am a physician in the public health service, and somebody presents to me a new drug. I can approve it now, although we do not know its full effects, and commonly we shall not know the full effects of a new drug for five to ten years after it comes out. If I approve it, and a series of tragedies such as this thalidomide tragedy comes, what will happen to me? I shall certainly be discharged, and I will be held up to public obloquy. The public at large will demand that heads roll. The penalties on me are very heavy indeed if I approve a drug I should not have. Suppose on the other hand, that it proves to be a fine drug, and in the long run its achievements are wonderful, but we do not know this yet. If I hold up the use of the drug for five years until all the results are in, a large number of people may die because it was not available. Their survivors will not write and complain that I did not approve the drug earlier. All the penalties are on me in making the mistake of approving the drug too early and none on the mistake of approving it too late. This combination of rewards and penalties . . . seems undesirable." [17] This simple application of the view that people (including government regulators) tend to have regard to their own self-interest leads to the conclusion that the regulation will result in considerable delay in the introduction of new drugs. Those of us who have seen the great improvements in health which have taken place in recent years as a result of the use of newly discovered drugs, particularly in the period since World War II, cannot feel that the new regulation may have done more harm than good. In this case, it so happens that by now there has been a quantitative study of the effects of the new drug regulation, by Professor Sam Peltzman of UCLA,[18] and it indicates that apprehension about the legislation was completely justified. The number of new drugs introduced each year on the average in the period 1963 to 1970 was about 40 percent of what it had been in the period 1951 to 1962, and a statistical investigation carried out by Professor Peltzman indicates that the whole of this decline was probably due to the new legislation. But he went further. Noting that while some of the drugs excluded from the market by the legislation would have been beneficial, others would no doubt have proved to be unsafe or no better than drugs already existing, Professor Peltzman proceeded to make a calculation of the probable benefits and costs of the new drug regulation. The result: the gains (if any) which accrued from the exclusion of ineffective or harmful drugs were far outweighed by the benefits forgone because effective drugs were not marketed. This conclusion was clearly foreshadowed by the essentially nonquantitative assessment of the probable results of the new drug regulation to which I drew your attention earlier. The economist who made this assessment was Professor Stigler. It represents a fine example of nonquantitative reasoning.

The results obtained by Professor Peltzman were not altogether surprising, since our normal theory would suggest that there would be a decrease (probably large) in the number of new drugs marketed, and, given the benefits which seem to be derived from newly discovered drugs, one would expect that this factor would dominate the results. But what was surprising (and our theory gives us no basis for expecting it) was that there is no strong evidence that the proportion of inefficacious drugs is substantially less in the smaller number of drugs marketed now than it was in the years before 1962. All this suggests, not that the decisions of doctors and patients about the use of drugs are correct, but that it is not easy to devise alternative institutions that will perform better.

This is, I believe, a common situation, although economists generally appear to have assumed otherwise. The reason for this sanguine attitude is that, while most economists do not ignore the inefficiencies of a market system, which, indeed, they are often prone to exaggerate, they tend to overlook the inefficiencies inherent in a governmental organization. It is therefore hardly surprising that economists in the last one hundred years or so have been led to support (or acquiesce in) an ever expanding role for government in economic affairs and have not felt a need for any serious investigation of the working of governmental organizations. What is wanted, if policy recommendations are to have a solid foundation, is to take into account both how a market actually operates and how a government organization does in fact carry out the tasks entrusted to it.

WHY HAS GOVERNMENT REGULATION FAILED?

Fortunately, the situation I have described does seem to me in process of change. Economists (along with others) are beginning to take a more critical look at the activities of government, and the kind of study which I have suggested as desirable is now being made. Certainly there have been more serious studies made of government regulation of industry in the last fifteen years or so, particularly in the United States, than in the whole proceeding period. These studies have been both quantitative and nonquantitative. I have referred to studies of the regulation of natural gas and drugs. But here have also been studies of the regulation of many diverse activites such as agriculture, aviation, banking, broad-casting, electricity supply, milk distribution, railroads and trucking, taxicabs, whiskey labeling, and zoning—I mention only studies with which I am familiar. There are doubtless many others. The main lesson to be drawn from these studies is clear: they all tend to suggest that the regulation is either ineffective or that, when it has a noticeable impact, on balance the effect is bad, so that consumers obtain a worse product or a higher-priced product or both as a result of the regulation. Indeed, this result is found so uniformly as to create a puzzle: one would expect to find, in all these studies, at least some government programs that do more good than harm.

In my paper on "Social Cost," I argued that, in choosing between social institutions, the decision should be based on how they would work in practice. I explained that there were costs involved in making market transactions and that consequently there were reallocations of factors of production which would, of themselves, raise the value of production but would not take place when the costs of the necessary transactions exceeded the gain in the value of production that would result. Such reallocations of factors can also, of course, be brought about by govern-ment regulation. Now government regulation also has costs—and gov-ernment regulators may have other ends in mind than raising the value of production. But the opportunity is there for government regulation to improve on the market. In my "Social Cost" paper, I said: "direct government regulation will not necessarily give better results than leaving the problem to be solved by the market or the firm. But equally there is no reason why, on occasion, such governmental administrative regulation should not lead to an improvement in economic ef-ficiency." [19]

My puzzle is to explain why these occasions seem to be so rare, if not nonexistent. One explanation would be that these studies happen to have involved cases in which there was a failure of government regula-tion and that further investigation will uncover many examples of success. But it is hard to feel much confidence in this explanation—the studies have been so numerous and their range so extensive, and some of the cases of failure are found where one might have expected success—for example, the control of monopoly, the regulation of drugs, or labeling, and zoning. Nonetheless, I am inclined to think that there may be something to this explanation and that if we looked more at government activities which affected directly the costs of carrying out market transactions we would indeed find cases in which governmental activities improved the situation. But I would not expect the inclusion of such cases to change the main conclusion, if indeed it is to be regarded as a qualification to it.

Another explanation for this record of poor performance of government would be that this is the way of the world—that the costs of government are always greater than they would be for the market transactions that would accomplish the same result. But I regard this as implausible.

I have come to the conclusion that the most probable reason why we obtain these results is that the government is attempting to do too much—that it operates on such a gigantic scale that it has reached the stage at which, for many of its activities, as economists would say, the marginal product is negative. We would expect to reach this stage if the size of an organization were allowed to expand indefinitely. I suspect that this is exactly what has happened. If further studies confirm that this really is the situation, the condition is one which can be cured only by a reduction of government activity in the economic sphere. This will not be easy to achieve, since it runs counter to prevailing attitudes. Oddly enough, the finding that many governmental activities do more harm than good is likely to be received sympathetically. It is common enough to read an article or the account of a speech of which the first part consists of a denunciation of the inefficiency and corruption to be found in the administration of some government program—but this is often followed by a second part which draws our attention to some pressing social problem coupled with the proposal that the government set up a new program or agency or expand an old one to deal with this problem. To ignore the government's poor performance of its present duties when deciding on whether it should or should not take on new duties is obviously wrong (old duties were once, in the main, new duties). But the sanguine view of what the government will accomplish induced by this way of thinking tends to lead to an ever expanding role for the government in economic affairs (and has done so). If I am right that the attempt to carry out these new activities leads to the government performing worse those that it is already undertaking, the continued expansion of the government's role will inevitably lead us to a situation in which most government actitivies result in more harm than good. My surmise is that we have reached this stage.

A POLICY RECOMMENDATION

This makes an economist's task in one respect easy and in another difficult. It becomes easy because at the present time the advice that has to be given is that all government activities should be curtailed. Our task is made more difficult because our experience with the present overexpanded governmental machine may not give us much indication of what tasks the government should undertake when the sphere of government has been reduced to a more appropriate size. But perhaps I exaggerate the difficulty. The move to a smaller government is hardly likely to be swift—and we will gradually be able to accumulate the information needed to discover what functions should be left to the government.

But all this assumes that the investigations of economists will, as Professor Stigler claims, in the end have a decisive influence on public policy. Whether the economist will be more successful in limiting the role of government than he has been in policies directly concerned with the operation of markets and the pricing system remains to be seen. But as I have indicated, even a modest success is not to be despised.

NOTES

1. Milton Friedman, "The Methodology of Positive Economics" in *Essays in Positive Economics* (1953), p. 5.
2. Edmund W. Kitch, "Regulation of the Field Market for Natural Gas by the Federal Power Commission," *Journal of Law and Economics* (October 1968), p. 243.

3. Edmund W. Kitch, "The Shortage of Natural Gas," Occasional Paper of the University of Chicago Law School, No. 2 (1971).

4. Adam Smith, *The Wealth of Nations* (Cannon edition, 1904), Vol., p. 25.

5. *Id.* at 27-28.

6. *Id.* at 28.

7. *Id.* at 35.

8. Edwin Cannan, "Why Some Prices Should Rise," in *An Economist's Protest* (1927), pp. 16-17.

9. *Id.* at 18.

10. *Id.* at 23.

11. Frank H. Knight, "The Role of Principles in Economics and Politics," *American Economic Review* (March 1951).

12. *Id.* at 2.

13. *Id.* at 4.

14. George J. Stigler, "The Economist and the State," *American Economic Review* (March 1965), p. 1.

15. *Id.* at 12.

16. *Id.* at 16-17.

17. George J. Stigler, "The Formation of Economic Policy," in *Current Problems in Political Economy* (DePauw University), pp. 74-75.

18. Sam Peltzman, "An Evaluation of Consumer Protection Legislation: The 1962 Drug Amendments," *Journal of Political Economy* (September-/October 1973), p. 1049.

19. R. H. Coase, "The Problems of Social Cost," *Journal of Law and Economics* (October 1960), p. 18.